Best wishes
Ly...

Echoes In My Mind

Rare Welsh Bits

Lyn Clarke

To:- Cheryl, nice to meet you 10-11-15

Clarke Books
Anna Maria Island, Florida

Also by Lyn Clarke

Memoirs of a Welshman

Ramblings of a Welshman

Reflections of a Welshman

Amazing States

Clarke Books

Cover design and book layout by Blue Harvest Creative Concepts
Copyright © 2011 by Lyn Clarke
All rights reserved. Published by Clarke Books

Printed in the U.S.A.
First Printing in August 2011

Dedication

To Stoker Second Class Lyndhurst R. Clarke, my father, who so bravely died during World War II, on 22nd, November, 1943 while on duty with His Majesty's Royal Navy base at Lerwick in the Shetland Islands. His involvement in Operation Double Cross, which was pivotal in allowing the Germans to mistakenly think that the Allies would invade Norway, was small but vital. His boat MTB.686 was one of several that was used to ferry Norwegians from their homeland, to Lerwick, where they were trained as spies and returned to Norway where they were led to believed that the D-Day invasion was to take place. Obviously if they were captured and interrogated the details which they would reveal, to the enemy, would be the misinformation that would lead the Germans to believe that the Allies were to invade Norway. This in turn tied up sixteen divisions of men [250,000] that would otherwise have been available to repel the D-Day landing in the north of France, thus making that operation a more successful venture. This mind blowing game of deception cost this valiant man his life but, in the greater scheme of things, saved many thousands of the Allied troops from being slaughtered on the Normandy beaches.

My father was an ordinary working man who was thrust into this dreadful existence but, like many others, he rose to the challenge and did what had to be done. It was extremely sad to find out that he, and all his shipmates, had to die as a result of a calamitous accident and that the cause of the incident was kept a secret for so many years. However, in the final analysis it is gratifying to know that his death was not completely in vain as all the details laid out in the addendum in "Reflection of a Welshman" has outlined. Just weeks earlier, when his boat sank a German naval ship, they allowed all the German sailors to man their life boats and sail away to safety before sinking the vessel. Even in the depths of a chaotic war there was honor and such heroic acts went unheralded. After all, men are men no matter where they are from and they should be treated with dignity and respect. If wars teach us anything it is that no one should ever enter into it until all other options have been thoroughly explored. Mankind is too fragile to be put into the position of possible extinction because of the misguided views of a minority of people. Many noble races have been obliterated because of unrealistic religious views, the greed for land expansions and the absolute obsession for power. When family members are lost, in the manner that I lost my father, you realize that gaining territories in some distant unknown land is no substitute for the closeness of kin folk. Let us all remember, when the war drums beat again, that we do not have to accept the fact that we have no other option but to do this thing above all else. Too many brave young people have been returned home to be buried at the place where they were once at their happiest. Some, as in my father's case, were never brought home at all but stay in an oddly foreign and distant location. Amen.

One

The Tapestry Of Life

We were all poor growing up in Pontypool after World War II. Not that it mattered because we were all in the same boat. Surviving was an ongoing day to day chore but this didn't bother us kids as we were similarly afflicted. As long as we had food in our bellies and clothes on our backs, albeit hand-me-downs, our lives were bearable. Most of our pastimes were things that didn't cost anything to do but mainly kept us outdoors and healthy. I walked the mountains at the back of where I lived a good deal and found innumerable ways of entertaining myself. I would collect birds eggs and this meant that I had to be a good tree climber. Particularly when raiding crow's nests as these were often forty or fifty feet up in the trees. This explains why they call the lookout tower on old sailing ships the crow's nest. One wet day when I was descending from a crow's nest my footing slipped and I slid down a few feet before regaining my footing. Our practice back then was to carry the bird's egg in our mouths so as not to break them during the descent. Unfortunately on sliding I hit my chin on a branch and the egg broke in my mouth. I had to spit out the broken egg, shell and all, but I never went back up to the nest as the unwritten law was that you only took one egg from any birds nest. After successful climbs we would bring the eggs home for our collections and there we would put a pin hole in opposite ends of the egg and blow the yolk out before putting them into our collection box. It might all sound somewhat barbaric, in this day and age, but I can assure you that it was much better time spent than idly sitting in front of a television playing video games like our present day children. It's no wonder we were all skinny back then when compared to our modern counterparts. I never ever owned a push bike and so if I had an errand to run I did just that...I ran. Low and behold to this day I still only weigh 160 pounds and play soccer twice a week. At my tender age this is virtually unheard of and I will continue this until I am unable to do so any further.

On one of my rambles up at the Tranch and over Twm Barlwm I witnessed what I still think, to this day, was one of the most amazing sights that I have ever seen. I was almost all the way over the top of the mountain towards Pantygasseg when about one hundred yards up ahead I saw a sight that defied logic. A tree seemed to be totally on fire and yet nothing else around it was. It resembled the burning bush from the Charlton Heston film *The Ten Commandments* which really made the entire moment seem surreal. It had what appeared to be flames flickering all over it and, as a young boy, I just could not understand what I was witnessing. However as I approached nearer to the tree it became apparent what the quandary was. The whole tree, which was a lilac tree, was completely covered with literally thousands of Red Admiral butterflies. They were all basking in the sun whilst individually opening and closing their wings as is their normal habit. This involuntary movement of theirs was giving the affect of flames flickering and this mass of red butterflies was giving the appearance of fire. When I descended the mountain and told my friends about the vision they seemed not to grasp the uniqueness of the incident which left my some-what deflated and puzzled. As I sit here in Florida, all these many years later and as a man approaching old age, I still picture this incident and ponder on that amazing sight from all those years ago. Maybe this was a regular event rarely seen by mankind but the sheer luck of my stumbling upon it has stayed in my minds eye until this very day and likely will until it fades to black. Of a similar nature there is a tree here in Florida which reminds me of Wales. I do not know the Botanical name for it but it is commonly called the daffodil tree. In Spring it blossoms all over with flowers that resemble the bell headed daffodil, and being almost four thousand miles from home, this affords me a modicum of satisfaction in this semi-tropical landscape.

Could it be that back in my youth a child's life was more meaningful and teemed with pure, simple pleasures than now. Could it be that back then we were more in touch with such sights and the over powering delights that Mother Nature provided. In later years I brought my own two children up to appreciate the county side and the mountains. The many beautiful birds and wildlife that abound all around us and the clear fresh air that we need to survive as a healthy species. Both of my children, even in the middle of their life's span, still love to take long country walks and embrace rural pleasures. I also instilled in them the fact that we should only eat when our body clocks tell us and that four meals a day is not always necessary. The electronic age is producing a generation of over weight and, at times, grossly obese people who have completely lost touch with reality when it comes to food consumption. This is even the case in my own home town as well as here in America and this, in of itself, provides proof that this is a western world epidemic. As a whole we must remember that there are two types of hunger generated symptoms. One is starvation when a person absolutely must eat or die and the other is merely a yearning for the taste of food which, if ignored, will disappear. The habit of walking around with a soda type drink in one's hand is going to worsen the affect and this is even more dire if repeated while sitting at a desk all day or in front of a television or computer. Hopefully as a human race we will one day come to our senses and realize that if drastic action is not taken, to curb this trend, then the world will be a sadder place to live in. One famous dietician recently stated that if the human population continues to consume food, at current rates, we will require two more planets, the same size as our present Earth, to supply the food needed to sustain our greed. What a sad reflection on our society ! But I digress.

To further illustrate just how poor our family was back then I clearly remember another incident but for a more macabre reason. We had a she cat as a pet in those days and could barley afford to feed her. The cat quite often took care of itself and would catch mice and even the odd bird or two. Back then we could not afford to have it spayed and, inevitably, it turned up pregnant. My mother was single as my father never did return from the war [see dedication] and she had enough trouble feeding my sister and I. When the cat produced a litter of six kittens my mother was distraught. She was left with no other option but to drown them all in a bucket of water out in the back yard. I was there and watched her do it and, at the age of eight, I was quite horrified by the whole incident. Now before the moral majority gets up on their soap boxes to decry this act of self preservation it must be remembered that these issues were very different back then. When a pet dog became ill and the decision was between its life and a family eating, the dog died. It was more practical to get another dog than to pay out money and have human beings go without food. My mother was a nurse back then and she had encountered many more earth-shattering events in her lifetime than this occurrence. The situation, at the time, was crystal clear to her and she knew exactly what her obligations were. She put her two children's well being in front of an animal's need which, in those chilling times, was absolutely what needed to be done. My mother passed on about ten years ago but she taught me the importance of where a persons loyalties should lie and my choice will always be humans first and foremost over animals. It is now quite normal for people to spend monies on, not only sustaining pet lives, but even pampering their four legged friends with ridiculous humanistic obsessions. At a time when some people are two pay checks away from living in a cardboard box, other people have an impulse to waste hard earned monies on pets. In my case I feel that a good pet is one that lives outside and has a good work ethic. Of course, here in America, it would have to be large enough to fend off coyote attacks as this predator would like nothing more than to have a miniature pet for supper.

In a similar vein I went on a bus excursion to a seaside resort in South Wales called Porth Cawl with my mother and sister. It was a trip arranged by one of our local pubs and we were all dressed up in our Sunday best. It was about a three hour drive before motorways were built and we arrived about mid afternoon. Immediately, on getting off the bus, we were confronted with an elderly gentleman who had collapsed in the middle of the parking lot. With cell phones not yet invented, a man was sent to phone for an ambulance while in the mean time a group of onlookers stood aimlessly around. Without thinking I took off my brand new jacket and placed it, like a pillow, between the dirt floor and the ailing man's head. I did not think that anything was out of place until the whole incident was over and the man was taken away by ambulance. My mother took me to one side and gave me a good telling off for using the jacket, which was bought through a catalogue and was not yet paid for, as a pillow. This came as a total shock to me as I thought that I was acting in a Christian-like manner, as after all it was Sunday, and would be applauded by all and sundry. My mother felt that the family of the befallen man should have done what I did and not stood around like spare grooms at a wedding. After her initial anger was quelled she gave me a hug and bought my sister and I a large ice cream and took us to the fairground for rides. This incident still puzzles me a bit but once again, after my father's death, my mother was all about us as a beleaguered family and not much else was important to her. There is no moral to this story and so I guess you will each have to make of it what you can. I for one am certain that our life experiences make us who we are today. We now live in a world where, in most civilized places, opposing views are considered to be healthy. It takes all sorts of people and opinions to build a world and at least here in America freedom of speech, concerning opposing view points, is an important part of our Constitution.

On another occasion my Nana, whom I loved dearly, had arranged a day trip to Barry Island with her sister, my Great Aunt Sally. This was the only time that I can remember when my grandmother ever went more than a few miles away from her home town. My sister and I went to the pickup location to see them off and when they embarked onto the bus, I started crying uncontrollably. I was probably around nine or ten years old and I couldn't understand why Gran was leaving me. My sister was more stoic and did not shed a tear. Finally, my Nana asked the bus driver if he could squeeze me on because I wouldn't take up too much room and he agreed. My sister ran home to tell my mother that I had gone on the trip and mother was not pleased at all. It wasn't much of a day out what with me spending my time to two staid older ladies. They wore ankle length dresses, stockings and shoes which meant that they never even put their toes in the sea. They also had very little money between them and so fair rides were out of the question and the most I received, all that day, was an ice-cream. My mother was there to meet the bus when we returned and, by the look in her eye, she was madder than a wet hen. It was only after my Nana had pleaded my case that mother calmed down and I do believe that this act of kindness saved me from a severe whooping. Talk about *fools rush in where angels fear to tread*. The bond that I had with my grandmother was strong and this lasted until she died and still lingers in my mind to this day.

Looking back to growing up in Wales I recall that we had a family doctor who smoked like a chimney. When I visited his surgery for consultation he would chain smoke while inquiring what was wrong with me. He always had a cigarette hanging from the corner of his lips and would cough up a lung from time to time. His face was wrinkled, his lips and fingers were stained from nicotine and he resembled an unmade bed with clothes that wreaked of smoke. Here was a man in the position to advise people how to have a healthy lifestyle but he was screaming out the opposite message. If a man who should know better cannot help himself then it is indeed a powerful drug to be avoided at all cost. It was made obvious to me that if people continued to inhale cigarette smoke then they are doomed to die from it at some future point. Perhaps this situation was a pivotal turning point in my life and the probable reason why I never took up smoking. For those who have, you had better wake up and smell the roses and stop inhaling the smoke.

Two

Circumstances Best Forgotten

My mother's mother, Nana, introduced my sister and I to Saint David's Presbyterian Church on Osborne Road when we were roughly seven and six respectively We attended Sunday School and after a few years she started to take us to the evening church service as our mother worked at the hospital at night on the weekends. Afterwards we would stay at her house and went to regular school straight from there the next morning, allowing mother to get some well-deserved sleep. At most of the Sunday evening services we would have our regular preachers but when they needed time off, for what ever reason, we would have lay preachers and these would come from far and wide. Our preachers were fairly mild-mannered in comparison to some of the laymen who tended to preach the Welsh fire and brimstone versions of the bible. They were in fact what we termed as *Bible Thumpers* because they were extremely animated and would even cry real tears during their stirring accounts of what otherwise would be quite ordinary stories. On one particular Sunday evening our church brought in this layman from the deepest darkest part of West Wales. He spoke in English but his Welsh accent was so thick you could cut it with a knife. This

14

rendered him barely audible at times and to top it off he had a pronounce stammer which increased as did the zeal of his story telling. My sister and I were quite impressionable at that age and when the layman first stammered it peaked our interest. We began to smile back and forth at each other but as the intensity of the sermon increased so did the stammering and my sister and I began to snicker. As the lay preacher became more and more animated we began to openly laugh until we reached a crescendo of guffaws with, by now, tears running down our cheeks. Our grandmother was mortified at our uncontrollable behavior and I swear, that if she wasn't so embarrassed, she would have dragged us outside and given us a severe whooping. Well that cured Nana of taking my sister and I to the Sunday night service. That stammering lay preacher probably saved us from any further strange encounters of the religious kind. From that night on we spent our Sunday nights running the streets with our friends or watching our favorite television shows. I guess there is a bright side to all situations if you diligently search for it. I quit attending all forms of church at fourteen years of age when a senior member tried to tell me that he had physically sat and talked to his father who had died twenty years earlier. The mind is a powerful thing and can persuade believing souls that they can actually do the impossible. Good luck to all those people who so believe, but I for one, will remain neutral on this issue.

The Salvation Army has my greatest admiration as being one of the most sincere forms of religious and benevolent practices. They are one of the few charities that I will always give to as they really do use the money for the good of other less fortunate people. One night, back in England, when I found myself without a bed to sleep on, I knocked on their hostel door and was taken in without any qualms or questions. This was many years ago but for a pittance I received a bed and breakfast and all that I had to do was wash a few dishes. I suppose one of the best things about joining the Sally Army is that they will teach you how to play a musical instrument. This explains why each unit of this organization has their own brass band which roams the local streets playing their hymns for all to hear. Unfortunately for them, one Sunday morning around 11:00 AM, their band stopped on the corner of King Street and South Avenue right under my mother's bedroom window. As usual she had just come off a twelve hour shift at the hospital and was trying to get some shut eye. After a few of their favorite hymns and just as the music reached its crescendo, my mother's bedroom window flew open and a stream of abuse came gushing forth. The band faltered to a halt, sounding like a deflated balloon, then they straggled off in some disorder to another location with their tails between their legs. Considering they carry the name "Army" in their title, they sure beat a hasty retreat that day and I don't believe that they ever played within four streets of my mother's house from that day forward. Back then the whole incident was quite embarrassing for me but looking back, from a safe distance, it all seems quite humorous now. The strange thing was that many years later and after my mother had retired from the nursing profession, she quite often would attend the Salvation Army's Christmas Concerts. With all her anger well and truly buried she put aside all her misgivings and enjoyed their company and hospitality. As the old saying goes "there is none so blind as those who do not want to see." Yes, my mother was a piece of work but she was the best mother that I ever had. The Dragon Lady, as she was so often referred to, roars no more but the strange thing is that she left her mark. Some people leave their impression for being good and others leave their impression for being bad but possibly the worse thing is when you leave no impression at all. It is almost as if you were never here at all and that, as they say, is a crying shame.

When I was fifteen my sister was dating a guy who was a lorry driver and worked for Sid Richardson who had a huge green grocery business in Pontypool Market. That year, during the school holiday, he let me go with him on pickup and delivery trips. We would drive around picking various vegetables from local farms and we would also go to major fruit markets like Newport and Cardiff. These were exciting trips for me and although I helped with the loading and unloading I wasn't officially paid. Obviously I had all the fruit that I wanted to eat and sometimes my lorry driver friend would slip me a small amount of cash which I thought was great. I enjoyed moving around and not being in one place all the time and I also liked the fact the no-one was looking over my shoulder to continually monitor what I was doing. The whole thing gave me a sense of freedom and this might have been what steered me towards being a salesman, ten years later, when I left the factory life style for ever. We went down to Cardiff one day to the biggest fruit market that I had ever seen in my life. My buddy was walking around talking to all the fruit vendors and checking out their prices before deciding from who he was going to buy. At the same time he was picking up various fruits and biting into them to test their freshness and firmness. This seemed a great idea to me and so, not having seen that my buddy had moved further on, I picked up a peach and sank my teeth into it. Before I had swallowed that first bite an enormous man came from out of nowhere and picked me up and shook me as though I was a rag doll. I was so shocked that I spit out the delicious piece of peach as though it was poison. While still holding me in a state of suspension the vendor threatened me to within an inch of my life if I ever stole from him again. At this time my buddy had realized that I was not with him and, on looking around, spotted the situation that I was in and my impending doom. He rushed over and told the distraught vendor that I was his assistant at which point he lowered me to the floor and straightened my dishevelled shirt. With a big grin the vendor apologized and said that he had mistakenly thought that I was one of the local street urchins who would sneak into the market and try to steal his wares. He was a big, strong man and one punch from him would have put me in Cardiff General Hospital for a few days. I was still trembling with fright about forty minutes later as we drove out of the market. My buddy got a lot of miles out of that story when we returned to Pontypool and for weeks after that he would ask me if I would like a peach. This was his private little joke at my expense and his way of keeping the incident alive. Whenever we went to a market, from then on, I made sure that I knew where he was at all times. Being shaken by a three hundred pound gorilla is no joke and should be avoided at all costs.

At nineteen I left home for good. My decision was made at a time when I had just broken up with a woman who was my first true love. Somewhere in the back of my mind I thought that I was man enough to make this sacrifice and that absence would make the heart grow fonder. I convinced myself that if I went away for a couple of years and grew up, then I could return a better person and hopefully pick up where I had left off with the love of my life. Well things did not work out that way at all and I liked my new life style so much that I never ever return to live back in South Wales. I had a good job prospect and at my tender age I had joined an excellent rugby club which was the other love of my life. I was outwardly tough but inside I was still very sentimental and at times home sick. Never the less I carried on with a stiff upper lip and convinced myself that I was man enough to continue regardless of all past associations. This I managed quite well from the September of that first year up until Christmas when the rugby club had a big party at the Oval Sports Center in Bebington. This was the first time in my life that I had been away from home at Christmas and everything went just fine until midnight when everyone began hugging and kissing and wishing each other well. Now I had been drinking quite a bit that night and all of a sudden I was overcome with emotion and like a stupid boy I began to cry. All my new friends and their girl-friends were trying to console me but it was all for naught. The more they tried to console me the worse I became until in the end I had to walk outside and just let it all out and have a good old fashioned sob. This seemed to do the trick and I returned to the party to loud cheers from my new rugby mates and a goodly sum of affection from a slew of single girls that were only too pleased to shower me with their love and attention. I was pretty embarrassed about my show of immaturity but the young ladies seemed to like the fact that I showed less than manly traits and this set me in good stead for dates for the next few weeks. Some of the more sinister of the male rugby clan brought the incident up from time to time in a derogatory manner but this didn't phase me one bit. This was far outweighed by the response from the female side of the equation which made the men's snide comments too far out in left field to even take seriously. Every now and again I wonder what my life would have been like if I had returned to South Wales. Well, I firmly believe that I would not have done half of the exciting things that I have accomplished in my life. It isn't Wales' fault, it is that I had developed an appetite to accomplish more and different goals and these opportunities did not exist in that part of the world. I had now grown up and my interests had moved away from the traditional ones that I had been brought up with. Let's face it, most people only find fame within a ten mile radius of where they were born and so when a person moves away from his natural environment he becomes increasingly influenced by the pattern of life which exists in the new region where he now resides. It is as simple as that and from here on it was all going to be sex, hugs and sausage rolls, baby!

Probably the most disturbing incident in my whole life, up to this very day, was when my first wife's father passed away. He was a cantankerous old Liverpool geezer and I seriously think that somewhere, along the way, he must have suffered a mild stroke. Some of the things that he did were totally bizarre and in the last year of his life he wanted to holiday in Spain but his wife refused to go with him because she was apprehensive about his odd behavior. When she would not go with him he advertised in the local newspaper for anyone to share this trip and a young lady, who worked with my wife, unwittingly answered the advertisement. This was all quite embarrassing for his whole family but he was determined to go and eventually that's exactly what he did by himself. He never returned alive from Spain as he collapsed at the dinner table one night, right in front of all the other guests in the restaurant. Apparently the hotel where he stayed had about a hundred steps leading from the beach up a cliff to its front door. After climbing these steps, on an extremely hot day, he had a heart attack in a most public of circumstances. This must have been very astonishing for all the other holiday makers and probably put a crimp in what should have been a joyous occasion. In Spain, the custom is to bury the dead within twenty four hours and it took a good deal of negotiation and money to prevent this from happening. His body arrived home about a week later in a lead-lined coffin but my mother-in-law would not believe that he was in the coffin and wanted it opened before his remains were buried. The undertaker pleaded with her not to do this but she was adamant. She, however, was not brave enough to view the body herself and so that task, unfortunately, fell to me. When the lead seal was broken a rush of the most foul smelling air gushed out and this was so obnoxious that I almost threw up right there and then. I viewed the body and I could barely make out it was him as the flesh had turned black and looked like leather. I told my mother-in-law that it was most definitely him, just to ease here mind, and the undertaker closed the coffin. I could not get that smell out of my nostrils and I had to walk to the far end of the yard, so that I could take deep breaths, to allow me to regain my posture. I have heard recently, during an infamous, local televised trial an argument concerning if the smell in the trunk of a car was a dead body or rotting pizza. I can vouch for the fact that nothing smells like the putrid, distinctive odor of a corpse. Even in the heat of Florida nothing can smell so bad as the remains of a dead body. The quotation in Shakespeare's Hamlet that "Something stinks in the state of Denmark" was never so true.

Three
Incidents and Accidents

I was married at the age of twenty four and was the proud father of a little girl at twenty six and a little boy at twenty eight. For the first two years of married life we rented an apartment on Spital Road in Bromborough, Cheshire which was on the top floor of a three-storied house. When the kids came along this proved to be too much work and so we had to look for somewhere else. We bought a house in Bebington at 38, Acreville Road and settled in very nicely. It was an attractive tree lined road and all of our new neighbors seemed friendly. There was a nice group of children in that street and as our kids began to grow up there was always someone out there for them to play with. One day my wife asked me if I would remove a long old curtain rail, which was situated the length of the living room picture window, as she wanted to put up a more contemporary version. It didn't seem that big of a deal and so one day, when she went shopping, I decided to give her a nice surprise and set about taking the old curtain rail down. I don't know who put the old rail up but it was as sturdy as a rock. I worked furiously to get it down but the son-of-a-gun would not budge. Finally, I gave it a huge tug and it let loose with a vengeance. I was standing on a ladder and when the swine rail broke free so did I. The ladder toppled over backwards sending me and the rail flying. At right angles to the wall of our living room we had a divider which we used as shelving and on which we kept all of our crystal glass wear. Me and the ladder hit the divider which was now also in motion and we all ended up in a heap on the floor. There was broken furniture and shattered glass all over the place and I considered myself very lucky not to be seriously injured. Alas, all the glasses, which I had brought back from various European trips, were in total ruin. As good luck would have it my wife did not return home for several hours which afforded me ample time to clean up the mess and finish putting up the new and modern curtain rail. When my wife finally arrived home I immediately showed her the new picture window accessory which please her no end. It took several more days before I could pluck up enough courage to tell her about the erstwhile crystal glasses which were no longer listed amongst of our prized possessions.

I decided one day that what we needed in our dining area, of the same room previously mentioned, was more light and to this end I purchased two very attractive wall mounted lights. There were wall plugs located in two convenient places which I decided would be the exact spots where my wall lights should be mounted. Now I am not very enthusiastic about dealing with electricity but I figured that it should not be too difficult to unwire the two plug points and replace them with the wall lights. Again, because of my wife's apprehension about my ability to deal with household chores, I decided to keep this little project to myself. Once again I chose a day when my wife was to leave the home to go shopping. I switched off the electricity at the mains, just like a professional, unwired the plug points and rewired the wall lights. Then, with a drum roll rattling in the back of my mind, I switched the main supply, which was located in the hallway, back on. There was a God Almighty bang and when I re-entered the dining room both of the wall lights were crumpled up in the middle of the floor. I had inadvertently wired them up backwards which left black burn marks on the walls and some severely wounded wall lights. With time on my hands I cleaned the walls, replaced the plug points and sent for a friend of mine who was a certified electrician. By the time my wife returned home from shopping the job was done and the electrician and I were out on the patio having some beers. I showed her the new wall lights and she was delighted, if you'll excuse the pun, and proud of her handy-man husband. Some months later, while we both were in the euphoria of alcohol, I confessed the whole fiasco to her and having selected the appropriate time she took it all in good humor. My enthusiasm for becoming the perfect husband was forever quelled and, hence forth, the proper artisan was hired for each individual chore.

During all this mayhem my main interest, outside of the home, was playing rugby. I was playing for Port Sunlight Club's first team and immensely enjoying the games and the post match parties and I was easily persuaded to stay later than I should at these events. On one such night the tales of that days battle became embellished to the maximum as we regaled ourself with praises and glories. About 8:00 PM the phone rang at the club house and it was my wife inquiring at what time I would grace her with my presence. She also said that my dinner was ready to which I replied that I would be a little while yet and for her to keep my dinner warm in the oven. The receiver on the other end was abruptly replaced with a resounding click ringing in my ear. About another hour later I bade my adeaus, to all and sundry, and wended my way home. When I arrived at the house my wife was watching television and at my bidding she retrieved my dinner from the oven and placed it in front of me on the table where I was by now sitting. On the plate was a burnt mass of indistinguishable food all crisp and black with an odor strong enough to floor a mule. I inquired of her as to what this burnt offering was, to which she replied that it was the salad which she had prepared and which I had instructed her to put in the oven. From that day forward if I ever received a similar phone call where food was debated, I always asked what was the specific product to be served up for dinner. My wife had made her point and had indeed gone up in my estimation. Of course all the other rugby wives were made aware of this cunning ploy and I was the butt of many a joke surrounding this matter. It was a typical "If you live by the sword you may die by the sword" moment.

Recently on a visit to the Wirral area of Cheshire I was staying at the Bridge Inn Hotel in Port Sunlight Village. This conjured up a myriad of bygone memories because in the highlight of my rugby playing career it was at this location that I partied the most. This, in the late seventies and early eighties, was the local Saturday night hot spot and was a popular watering hole for many of that areas top rugby players and their female companions. I use the term companions because some of us were married, some engaged and others just dating. I guess the word today would be partners but for some reason I have difficulty in using this word in a suitably constructed sentence. Anyway, Harry Burrows, Bary Roberts, Pete Metcalfe, Joe Byrne, Alan Burley, Alec Mc Diarmid, Pete Lister, Mike Green and Alan Haig were some of these reprobates and it was great to see a good few of the same people, thirty odd years later, when we all met up again at the Three Stags last month. While at the same afore mentioned Inn on my latest stay I wanted to put money on a horse that I had been advised to bet. On inquiring as to the nearest betting shop I was told that it was located in Lower Bebington. On finding the shop and placing my bet I discovered that it just so happened to be virtually next door to The Wellington pub, known to the locals as The Welly. I could not miss the chance of having an alcoholic beverage at this oasis in a desert of trouble and strife. While standing there, drink in hand, I was pondering on the nearness of this pub to my old house on Acreville Road. All of a sudden a crazy thought came into my head. Why not walk on over a few streets, knock on the door of my old house and introduce myself. In five minutes flat I found myself standing at the door filled with trepidation. As an elderly lady opened the door I said that I used to live in this particular house thirty five years ago. A smile came across her face and she asked if I was a Mr. Clarke who she and her husband had bought the house from. Guilty as charged.

She kindly invited me in and gave me a full tour of every room in the house which, for some unknown reason, brought a lump to my throat. Where we had a cement slab outside of the picture window they had added a conservatory which made the house look much bigger. They had also took the kitchen wall back level with the conservatory doubling the size of it. They had brought the garage area forward down the drive more and all in all they had done a bang up job on improving the old house. Sadly the ladies husband had passed away around ten years earlier and she had lived on alone in that house but she assured me that she had enjoyed her many years at that location. I am so glad that I chose to do this as it seemed to quench my curiosity concerning the well-being of this old and revered friend. I gave her my business card and told her to feel free and phone me at any time she desired but to date I have not heard from her. On leaving I walked back to The Welly, watched my horse lose and then walked back to the Inn for dinner. Off-the-cuff decisions, like this, often turn out better than those that take forever to arrange. I think that in these cases the expectancy of failure is forefront in one's mind and when things do actually work out for the better it is like an unplanned bonus. Another saying springs to mind and that is "fools rush in where angels fear to tread " For a Frenchman this would be considered the road to Rouen!

The reason, as a teenager, that I found myself in Cheshire was because I was transferred by Girling Ltd of Cwmbran to work at their new factory which was being opened up in Bromborough. I worked on the Wirral, for this company, for the last two years of my apprenticeship and for a further three years as a Methods Engineer. At the age of twenty four I left Girling's for good and became an Industrial Salesman for the rest of my working life, both in Britain and America, until I finally retired. However, before my leaving Girling's an extremely embarrassing incident occurred. We office people started work at 8:00 AM and had to clock in every morning, to register the time that we arrived at the factory. Quite often there would be a last minute mad flurry of activity as the stragglers dashed in to beat the eight o'clock deadline. On this particular morning I had just clocked in when I looked up to see one of the office secretaries come gingerly into view. She was walking, as fast as she could, in a most peculiar manner and as she became about level to where I was standing her panties dropped down around her ankles. She calmly bent down and picked them up, clocked in and scurried away to the ladies rest room. She obviously knew that her elastic had snapped and was hoping that she could make it past me before the inevitable happened but she did not. However, the aplomb with which she performed, under great stress, was to be admired. As that day went on I mused with the vision of her plight and wondered if women ever carry a spare pair, in their purse, to enable them to continue with their daily routine. Whenever this eighteen year old young lady passed me, in the factory, she would color up and blush something awful. She could never look at me straight in the face but would stare into space with a vacant far off look. To face me would be to admit that the incident really did take place but if she didn't acknowledge me she could pretend that the whole horrendous episode was a figment of her own imagination.

Lyn at age nine

Lyn the matador

Lyn after a rugby game

Lyn in Spain

Four

Strange Encounters

I had lived in South Wales for the first eighteen and a half years of my life and in Cheshire, England for about the same period of time. I was now off to America where I would live for the rest of my life up to the present date. I arrived in Detroit, Michigan in the September of 1976 and my wife and two children came in the April of the following year. Talk about culture shock. Life in America was much faster and more exciting in every aspect you could think of. I made a good deal of friends, as is my trait, and always had something going on both at work and play. A few of my old friends came out to see me in the states from time to time and for a while I always seemed to be at Detroit Metro Airport to meet someone or other. On one such incident I met a famous lady tennis player from England. Her name was Sue Barker and she was standing all alone near the baggage carousel area and looking completely lost. I engaged her in conversation and she said that someone was supposed to meet her and take her to the hotel where she was to stay during her visit. I chatted with her and tried to make her feel comfortable until her contact arrived to collect her. It was a pleasant encounter and I felt that she appeared to be thankful for the small amount of time when I kept her safe and at ease in a foreign land. I did not feel entitled to ask the nature of her visit but I am sure it was successful. She was a beautiful, polite and gracious person. She is still often seen on British television commentating on the big tennis events, especially Wimbledon, which usually takes place in England during the last two weeks of June. On another late night I was at the same airport to pick up some-one or other and was standing on the sidewalk outside of the baggage claim area when three very tall skinny African-American ladies, all wearing expensive fur coats, hurried by. It took me a minute to get my head around just who they were. When the penny finally dropped I realized that they were the Pointer Sisters who, at that time, were at the height of their careers.

The most unusual event that I encountered at Metro Airport was late one evening when I was in the arrival area waiting to meet a business associate who was due to get off a plane from London. That night there were many more people in the arrival area than I had ever seen before. A large percent-age of the awaiting crowd were of Middle-Eastern origin and were in an excited state almost reaching fever pitch. I lived, at that time, in the city of Dearborn, to the south east of Detroit, and the eastern part of that city had more of these people than anywhere outside of the Middle East itself. All of a sudden they all rushed to the foot of the escalator and there ascending, as if from Heaven, was this distinguished looking man dressed in an eastern religious styled outfit. He looked so dignified as he ascended at a slow pace never moving from the stair that he was standing on. When he reached the bottom of the escalator he was immediately enveloped by his adoring fans. He was presented with gifts and flowers and the whole scene looked right out of a Rudyard Kipling novel. Obviously this man, of great importance, was allowed to deplane first and finally his adoring fans whisked him away to some unknown destination. About five minutes after the throng had dispersed my business associate met up with me and he was completely oblivious of all the hoopla that had preceded him. It was a number of years later that I found out who this adored man was. A war had broken out in Lebanon and, on this particular night I was watching the International News on television. They were discussing this pivotal event and suddenly they showed some film clips of different people being interviewed and there he was. He was the religious leader of the Lebanese Shiite Moslem sect called Hasballah. The war that had erupted was between the Shiite and Sunni religious sects of that country and this man, being the leader of one of them, was in a position of prime importance. The Moslem religion, incidently, came about some five hundred years after Christianity and was started by the Prophet Mohammed. When he died one sect wanted his son to take over as his religious heir and the other sect wanted his nephew to succeed him. Since that time in history the two sects have been divided and from time to time the whole disagreement boils over into a bloody and vicious war. When I met this man he appeared to be in his late twenties and, by my estimation, he now has to be around sixty years of age and as long as he lives he will always be the leader of this distinct group of people. I played soccer in the Detroit area with a good few Lebanese players but they were all Christians and before coming to America they also had been involved in wars albeit this time between their religion and Moslems. They would proudly show off their bullet scars and war wounds when asked and they would be enraged if anyone ever referred to them as Arabs. Such is the complex nature of the country of Lebanon.

I was flying out of that same airport several years later when I encountered another bizarre incident. I was making a business trip down to Texas and it was going to be a long day. The flight was delayed and the boarding process seemed to take an eternity. We were finally loaded onto the plane and were preparing for take off when it became apparent that a passenger was missing. A man had told a flight attendant that his wife had left the plane to smoke one last cigarette and I guess she thought that she could just step outside of the plane and light up. However, smoking is not allowed in the walkway and so she ambled up to the gate area only to be told that she could not smoke there either. She then wondered away from the gate area to find an area where she could smoke not giving a care about the almost two hundred passengers waiting on the plane. The air crew decided that she would have to be left behind and began to close the doors in preparation for take off. In the meantime the woman's husband, who was not a well man, was so distraught that he looked like he was just about going to have a heart attack. At this point the crew members were asking him to get off the plane so that he and his wife could catch a later flight but the man appeared to be physically incapable of moving himself. At the height of all this fuss and bother Queen Cleopatra, his wife, decided to grace us with her presence. She entered with such an air of disbelief and an attitude of "I could care less" and she could not understand what all the commotion was about. She had held the plane up for some forty or more minutes, almost gave her husband a heart attack and caused countless other passengers the possibility of missing their connecting flights but she could not see anything wrong. Now that it just about the height of narcissistic indulgence. How anyone could be so self absorbed not to consider any other person, not even for one minute, is about as rude as can be. I only hope that at sometime in the future, she will be treated in a similar fashion. Perhaps when she is left in a dire situation, and the person she so desperately needs, decides to step out for a cigarette and leaves her in the lurch. Most women that I have met in life are kind and considerate and the only exceptions that I have ever found to the contrary are women who overly indulge in love, alcohol or cigarettes. Along the path of life why do I always find the psychopath?

When I first arrived in the Detroit area I met some real characters. This one particular guy was always bitching about how times were tough and he could hardly make ends meet but he always appeared to be dressed smartly and never was short of a few spare dollars in his pocket. One day I bumped into him while I was out shopping and I asked him if he wanted to go for a few brews. He said that he would meet me later at Miller's Bar on Michigan Avenue but first he had an errand to run. As we parted he garbled something, which sounded to me like he was going to a shoe exchange. I shook my head trying to imagine what I thought he had just said but it made no sense to me at all. I went on about my business and around 5:00 PM I was sitting on a stool in Miller's when my buddy strolled in. He jumped up on the stool next to me and got stuck into the cool beer which I already had sitting for him on the bar. We got to chit-chatting about our days and then I said that I mistakenly thought that he said that he was going to the shoe exchange. He told me that was exactly what he had said and he proved this fact by showing me the shiny new pair of black Florsheims that he was sporting on his feet. I was still perplexed by all this and asked him to explain to me how this transaction took place. He said that he quite simply walked into a charity store with an old pair of shoes on his feet. He would then examine all the resale shoes and if he came across a pair in his size that was better, he would just simply exchange them for his old pair, and stride out the door with not so much as a backward glance. Well I must say that I just sat there speechless for a few minutes because, quite frankly, I had never heard anything like that before in my life. Then I said that I hope that he did not frequent any other exchange shops which specialized in underwear and such or

I would have to view him in a completely different light. He assured me that his fetish only extended to shoes and that he had no plans to increase his wardrobe. Thank God for that. I mean a dead man's lightly used shoes is one thing but other parts of the anatomy have to be treated with respect. About a year later this guy inexplicable disappeared from sight. Some people said that he had moved with a job to another State of the Union but I just have this lingering feeling that Someone on High took a dim view concerning this matter and might have dealt some form of retribution. I mean just because you are paranoid it does not mean that someone is not following you.

At this time I lived at an apartment complex called Woodcrest Villa right off Wayne Road in Westland, or as some folks jokingly called it Wasteland. On Friday nights I was in the habit of going to the Canadian Legion club over in the south part of Dearborn Heights. I would stay there until around 11:00 PM and then I would drive back and have a few cocktails at a bar, called Chatters about a half mile from where I lived. There was a woman who frequented this bar that for some reason took a real shine to me and made her feelings quite obvious. I was living with another desirable woman at that time and, although her advances were appreciated, I decided that retreat was the better part of valor, and rebuffed her impassioned pleas. After a month or so of this treatment she finally got the message and moved her designs to another guy and, although I missed her attention, it was for me a sensible solution to a growing problem. A month or so later I strolled into Chatters on a Friday night and the whole place was abuzz with excitement. One of the barmaids beckoned me over and she grasped me close to her. She told me that the previous Friday night, when I was absent, that particular woman who had the hots for me, was with her latest assignation. At the end of the night they left together and were making out in his car in the parking lot. Out of nowhere the woman's estranged husband appeared and ambushed them, unloading a shot-gun into the car at point blank range. The guy put the car into reverse and squealed out of there like a bat out of hell. He was wounded but, alas, the woman was killed outright. I had the shivers just as if someone had walked over my grave and I left immediately. I went home to ponder on this event and my most prominent thought was "There but for the grace of God go I." I am not a wholly religious person but this was one time in my life when I think that I experienced divine interven-tion. This woman was a real good looker and was exactly the kind that I normally made a bee line for. She was a shapely, well-proportioned blonde with a great personality but there was something that told me to stay away and whatever that was could have saved my life. The ebb and flow of life and death moves in mysterious ways and I am a firm believer that when your time is up, there is nothing to be done about it. In days gone by Native American Indians, at a time when they felt that their life was at an end, simply walked out into the wilderness and sat down under a tree waiting for death to come. At this particular juncture of life my time was not due and so I lived to play another day. Some people call this fate or kismet but whatever it is I am grateful that my life was spared. There is probably nothing worse than a jealous and avenging husband with a loaded shotgun. This beauti-ful young woman's life was snuffed out in a second and her extraordinary good looks and vitality were gone forever. The road to romance can be fraught with danger and it is always best to air on the cautious side in matters of the heart. A good offer might come with a hidden agenda and this, in of itself, could lead to a catastrophic ending.

Five

On The Road Again

I had some real good times in Michigan and made some life-long friendships but around 1999 I had the chance to move south to the Sunshine State of Florida and I grasped it with both hands and run like a bandit. Not only did I move to Florida but I relocated myself to live on an island in the Gulf of Mexico. I was now living ocean side and drinking cocktails under the shade of a tiki hut. As a young man back in Wales I dreamed of wearing a Hawaiian-styled multi-colored shirt while sporting a healthy sun tan and surrounded by bikini clad maidens. I never ever really thought that this could happen but when it did, I took to that life style like a duck to water. In next to no time at all I was wearing flip-flops and sporting a shark's tooth on a gold chain around my neck. I let my hair grow longer than it normally would be and I completely immersed myself in the Island style of casual living. One of the great advantages of living in paradise is that I tend to run across many interesting and influential people. The other advantage is that I rarely ever meet anyone in a foul mood. On the contrary, most everyone is in a great frame of mind because they have the monies which are needed to visit or live here comfortably. The climate, of course, is conducive to healthy living and the availability of plentiful fish and fruit means that most locals look ship shape and happy. It is the definition of the difference between compatible and comparable, a slight but extremely important variation. How are you gonna keep them down on the farm after they've seen Paree?

At the midway point of winter in Michigan my soccer playing buddies from the Canton Celtics Club take a long weekend break and head south to play the Sarasota Football Club. At a time when cabin fever has become no longer tolerable, they make there way south by any available mode of transport. Two or three of them, who are financially strapped, usually end up sleeping at my house. I say "sleeping" as opposed to "staying" because they are rarely home during the daylight hours or appear after the local watering holes have closed. On one such trip it coincided with the Major Soccer League's Spring training camp at the Bollettieri Academy [now owned by I.M.G.] about five miles inland from my island home. We all went over to watch these professional practice matches and they are always very informative for us amateurs. I spotted a man sitting on an embankment writing notes to himself in a small note pad. I wandered over and plunked myself down near to him and struck up a casual conversation. After listening to his comments it became obvious that he was a soccer coach and he seemed to be eying up various players and their abilities. He was not too talkative and so, feeling that I had overstayed my welcome, I politely wished him good luck and moved on back to my Cantonites. They asked me who the guy was but all I could say was that he was a coach picking out players. Less than a week later, after my friends had returned to Michigan, I was watching the Sports News on ESPN when the new coach for the American National Soccer Team was announced. Yes, it was the very same tight-lipped acquaintance that I had met at the

Soccer Academy. His name was Bob Bradley and he took the USA National Team to the 2010 World Football Cup in South Africa. The American team was knocked out in the Quarter Finals by Algeria in extra time. England, incidently were also knocked out by Germany in the Quarter Final stage in regulation time. When I visit the United Kingdom some people over there ask me when is it that soccer is going to catch on in the USA. I have to remind them of the fact that the USA virtually knocked England out of the World Cup because the head-to-head game between them was tied. If England had won that game, and ultimately their division, they would not have had to face Germany so early in the elimination rounds. This, in turn, would have given them more games in which to formulate their team and their tactics which then would have given them a better chance to progress to the final stages. From past experience it has been proved that the longer a team stays in the competition, the better it progresses. If anyone wanted proof of that they only have to look at Italy who won this competition, eight years earlier, after almost being eliminated in the first round by a group of no hope players.

On weekends my wife, Sharon, helps to manage a small restaurant on our island called Paradise Café and when she is extremely busy I also lend a hand. The café has a nice eclectic group of employees and also has a loyal group of customers who frequent the breakfast and lunch scene which is a seven day a week event. During season, from November to the end of May the owner, Jackie, also opens three evenings a week for three-course dinners. Her food is not to be missed and some customers have travelled considerable distances to partake of her creative culinary offerings. A long-standing customer, a police sergeant from New York named Richard Westby, was unfortunately diagnosed with cancer and it was very sad for us to watch him slowly losing his battle. He loved motorbikes and to a lesser extent enjoyed golf and so to cheer him up, one of the waitresses, Amy, decided to give him a surprise. From another job that she worked at night she had become quite friendly with another man who had experienced a similar battle, with the same illness, and thus had travelled down the same dark road as the policeman was experiencing. This man was in remission from the disease and also was a golfer of some note and a Harley Davidson motor-bike enthusiast. This man was none other than the famous local born world renown golfer Paul Azinger. Paul had written and just released a book about his life and ultimately his battle...and victory over cancer. Amy arranged with him that, on a particular day and time when she knew that the unsuspecting policeman would be at the café, that Paul would arrive unannounced and present him with an autographed copy of his book. We all awaited the moment, with bated breath, as he roared up in front of the café on his powerful Harley. He walked in dressed in his leathers, not looking at all like a golfer, and walked over to the policeman's table. A look of total disbelief settled on the policeman's face as he could not take in what was unfolding before him. They sat together for awhile and although we left them alone, while they shared a conversation, I am sure that Paul imparted to him some encouraging words. Alas the policeman lost his battle and passed away around six months later. Paul had played for the USA in the 2008 Ryder Cup and the next time that I saw him was on the television one day when he was doing the background commentary on the 2009 Ryder Cup which the Americans won. The 2010 Ryder Cup was played out on my home territory at The Celtic Manor in Caerleon, South Wales. Before anyone tries to correct me and say that the venue is in Newport, I will remind them that when the venue was announced Newport immediately annexed Caerleon into it's borough. They then set about isolating Caerleon from this prestigious event and the businesses of that town from benefiting from all proceeds. As a footnote to this story I would just like to add that after the policeman passed away, his wife gave my wife, Sharon his Carlo Robelli six-stringed acoustic guitar in appreciation for all the kindness that she had shown during those difficult times.

Yet another person that I met at Paradise Café was an English gentleman named Freddie Fletcher. For the unini-tiated a fletcher is a man who used to attach the feathers required to make an arrow fly straight [another piece of useless information that can be used at social affairs in times of pregnant silences]. He was sitting outside under one of the sun umbrellas with his wife when, as is my want, for no particular reason I started up a conversation with him. I had absolutely no idea who he was but I heard his British accent and inquired where he was from. This led to him telling me that he had been the Chairman of Newcastle United Foot-ball Club and Glasgow Rangers F.C. He also told me that he had been instrumental in connecting these two prestigious soccer clubs with the Newcastle Ale Brewing Company who became the sponsor, for both clubs, for many years. Freddie is, of course, now retired from the football business, however in his time he was the vanguard and a guiding light for other clubs to follow. He left his mark on the football scene and will be remembered for sometime to come and it was my distinct pleasure to have made his aquaintance.

While recently in Caerleon I strolled into The Minstrel Arm, on the green, and unexpectedly became embroiled in watching a darts match between that establishment and a local Newport team. I have played some darts in my time and I was immediately impressed by a young lady on the visiting team. Her darts were thrown with vigor and accu-racy and, although she did not hit all her targets, there was something about her style that caught my eye. This young lady had recently been persuaded to take up the game again after a several year hiatus and she was slowly but surely finding her game again. At the age of twelve she was so good that she represented Wales in the All Ladies World Cup in Australia and her team unexpectedly won the championship. Her family could not afford to go and so it was left to other people to chaperone her and she returned less than happy with the whole affair. At thirteen she won the European Ladies Cup and at fourteen she won the Girls Youth World Masters event and was literally on top of the world. Then for a mixture of reasons she abruptly retired from the sport. The match which I witnessed, in the Minstrels, was a part of her resurgence back into the game of darts. She told me that she has lately taken up the game of pool and, even without seeing her play, I bet she is good at it. Oh, her name? Her name is Kimberly Lewis and I can tell you this because she gave me her personal permission to do so. In the past ten years I have witnessed several women pool players, from Britain, come to America and sweep the board so far as titles and money are concerned and I think that Kimberly could do the same if she has the determination to give it her best shot.

While I was in the UK people there were still bubbly over the royal wedding of Prince William and Kate Middleton. This event occurred less than a month before I arrived and so it was very much still in the minds of the people there as being a wonderfully happy day of celebration. I remember watching all the revelry on the television over here in Florida and thinking back to when I was in Wales the very day, in 1986, when Prince Charles married Diana Spencer who was lovingly known to all the people as Princess Diana. Having experienced that joyous event I could appreciate how the new generation felt about their recent royal wedding. However, back in America that day was not remembered as being a happy time. A devastating tornado had just literally wiped the town of Joplin, Missouri right off the face of the earth.

It must be a horrifying experience to be happily living in a town one day and find it completely gone the next. I think that of all the bad emotions that a human being can experience, this must be one of the worse. To lose family, pets, livestock, houses, cars and a lifetime of personal affects must feel like having your heart ripped out. I mean how do you go on or, even more depressingly, how do you start all over again. I pondered on the plights of two sets of people at totally opposite ends of the spectrum. In England, everyone was euphoric while, at that very same moment, others across the Atlantic Ocean were in the deepness of despair. It is sometimes a strange world that we live in and although I am completely aware that everybody cannot be happy all the time, perhaps someone up there could be a little more thoughtful and even out the highs and lows.

For instance, here on this island where I live, a woman hotelier has been missing for almost three years. A suspect, her new boy friend, is being held in jail for violating his probation on another crime of trying to burn down his previous girl friends house. It is suspected, by just about everybody, that he has murdered her but he will not talk and since her body has not been found he cannot be charged. Just the other day a guy, that I have played soccer with, found something of her's on his property virtually on the beach. Because of this the police have renewed the search and are digging up the beach in that area in the hope of finding her. A few months before she disappeared my wife and I sat at the same table as her at a mutual friend's dinner party. We shared some conversation over a few cocktails and have never set eyes on her since. Like everyone else who knew her we hope that she will be found so that she can be given a memorial service and a proper burial which she so justly deserves. A little help, from on high, would be greatly appreciated in this matter.

Six

On the Crest of a Wave

On the street where I now live, here on Anna Maria Island, I had a neighbor who was a retired Army Officer who serve his country while in different parts of Asia. He was pleasantly retired on his army pension and lived comfortably in a large three lot home. His house was the only building that stood between mine and the Intercoastal Waterway, which separates our island from the mainland of Manatee County. This man's family had lived on this island since the early days and his father was the first doctor in our town of Bradenton Beach. In fact the very house that I just mentioned was, in fact, the doctor's surgery for many of the early days in our city's history. My neighbor died about two years ago and his son and three other siblings immediately sold the long time family home for close to one million dollars. It was bought by a developer who immediately knock the house down and split the land back into three separate lots and began constructing three individual houses on it. Instead of one single level home they have now built two three storied homes with the third lot currently vacant until the housing market regains its strength. The homes are obviously brand new and of attractive designs and have given our little street a new air of prosperity. The one house was bought by a lady from Nashville, Tennessee and the second by a family from Pittsburgh, Pennsylvania. Our otherwise staid community has now taken on an air of well being and has attracted many new out of State visitors to eye our street as a good place to set up home. Of course, all this does wonders for my property and although I am not considering selling my house at this point in time, who can tell if the time and the price is right, perhaps I can be persuaded. The whole deal would, however, depend upon whether or not I could find a suitable place to move on to. Obviously, if a developer was to buy my property he would quite naturally level my existing home and build two large houses like the ones now standing across the street. In the realty business the key word is location...location...location. From that point of view I am sitting on a most desirable piece of property and even if the very worst scenario occurred and my house was destroy by a hurricane, I could sell the plot of land for twice what I paid for it twelve years ago. All this is a comforting situation in these times of uncertain trends and as I get older it gives me inner strength to know that I do not have to worry unduly about the future. My choice of locating to this particular spot becomes better and better as time goes by.

In recent years I have made the acquaintance of two new friends who are a cut above the norm. The one gentleman moved to this area from California and works in the field of Forensic Science and, by all accounts, is one of the leading lights in that complicated field of work. He has written papers on a specific area of that field and his work is often used and referred to by the Law Enforcement industry in many of their strange and difficult cases. I met this gentleman through playing soccer which just goes to prove what a mixed bag of individuals are attracted to that dignified sport. This man also lives directly across the Intercoastal from me and is only a two minute boat ride away. Outside of his house is docked his boat which in this case is a seventy four foot long two masted ketch which is one of the best boats it has been my good fortune to have been on. My wife and I were invited to sail on the Maya from the boat yard in Cortez Village over to this man's dock and it was exciting to say the least. When the boat was being lowered into the water all the customers from the Cortez Kitchen restaurant came out to take photographs of this magnificent sight. This man has an abundance of expensive toys in his life and even keeps kegs of Germany beer on board for the discerning drinkers like my good soccer buddy Enrico. This gentleman has brought a new dimension of fun into our lives and for that reason alone, is deserving of a special mention.

The second of the two new friends is a business man who has wheeled and dealt in many business segments but most of his time has been spent associated with the Agriculture Industry. He has invented a good number of machinery and implements which he has designed and sold to Third World developing countries. Unfortunately an unscrupulous employee of his, in a position of great trust, stole monies from him and bankrupted his thriving business. However, this never-say-die character has made an outstanding comeback and is on the verge of launching his new product, which if it takes off as it should, will revolutionize a particular segment of the Leisure and Outdoor Industry. It is a safety device which is simple and inexpensive to install on a pool's suction pump and has the capacity to save the lives of many innocent children. This in a market that has been unable to address this specific and dangerous problem in the past. I wish him well in his endeavors and I hope that this will allow him to return to the lifestyle that he so justly deserves. Good luck mate and, in sailing terms, may the wind be with you on your journey. Yet another soccer playing buddy of mine works for a Swedish company, based in Sarasota , that refurbishes teak boat decks. Obviously any boat which has teak decks is expensive and are owned by some of the wealthiest people on this planet. He told me, the other day, that he had just come back from Fort Lauderdale where he had worked for two weeks on a one hundred and sixty four foot long yacht which is owned by Johnny Depp. What a lucky Stiff to have a job like that and as much grog as you want to "splice the main brace" with.

Shortly after arriving on Anna Maria Island we used to frequent an old Florida styled bar called Key West Willey's. This is typical for bar names around here as we also have Rotten Ralph's, Hurricane Hank's, Skinny's, Slim's and assorted other colorful names which conjure up visions of our sub-tropical atmosphere. My daughter and her partner were visiting us, from England, and we were taking them around the local tourist traps and this was on the agenda. A woman, seated along the bar from us, ordered some oysters and I'll be damned if she didn't find a pearl in one of them. Now that about sums up how different living here really is. Now I am not saying that this sort of thing is a common occurrence but this type of event sure adds to the mystique and aura of living in these parts. The sights and sounds of this beautiful island are both breath taking and literally amazing. One of my joys of living here is to go over to the beach, about one hundred yards away, on most evenings at the setting of the sun to enjoy the cool night breeze and the spectacular show that Mother Nature provides. The colors are simply breath taking and with all the variety of island birds winging their way back to the Preserve, on Egmont Key, it is an event that I never tire of. Sometimes as the tip of the disappearing sun hits the horizon an elusive and rare neon green flash can be seen. This can only be seen with the naked eye and you must stare at it without blinking. These occasions are rare but very exciting and many people still think that it is a myth but I can assure you that it is real and I have witnessed this natural phenomena on countless occasions. So too has Captain Jack Sparrow and he would not tell an untruth now would he? A pirate once asked his blind pirate mate how he could detect what the value of the coins were being put into his beggars box. The blind one replied "Because I have a cute earring ."

Magazines and television travel shows in Europe are applauding the merits of this island which, up until now, has been the best kept secret in Florida and perhaps in America. Most days, at the Paradise Café, many different accents and dialects can be heard and this amplifies the fact that my decision to move her was one of, if not the best, decisions that I have made in my entire life. I get withdrawal symptoms whenever I have to leave the island for any length of time and on returning it is as if someone has lifted all the cares of the world from my mind

At least I can think of one trip off the island that wasn't too painful. My wife and I have two major book selling events per year. One of these is our trips back to the Old Country and the other is attending the Annual Welsh Convention which is moved around the United States from year to year. Coming up this year it is to be held in Cleveland, Ohio but we have attended this gathering in Alexandria, Virginia, Chicago, Pittsburgh and Portland, Oregon. These events bring together Welsh people and people of Welsh descent from all over the USA and Canada and is a joyous occasion. Last year this prestigious event was in Portland and after four days of hard work my wife and I decided to head for the Pacific Northwest Coast which is both rugged and beautiful. I have always been a history buff and American events like The Indian Wars, the Louisiana Purchase and the American Civil War capture my imagination. Another great event which shape the destiny of the USA was the Lewis and Clark Expedition in the early eighteen hundreds which solidified America by exploring and mapping the lands west of the Mississippi River and all the way out to the Pacific Ocean. When this expedition was completed, America had virtually doubled the size of its land mass. It only took Texas to join The Union, after the Battle of the Alamo, for the United States to stretch from sea to shining sea [the Atlantic to the Pacific.]

With my name being Clarke I just had to go to Astoria, Oregon to visit the fort where this expedition spent their first winter on the Pacific coast. Being the joker that I am I told the buck-skinned, coon-hatted fort guide that my name was Clarke and I asked if any of my kinfolk had "come through these here parts." He really got a kick out of that remark and gave a personal and detailed guide through the entire fort. What brave men these pioneers were. All they knew was that the Mississippi River obviously arose somewhere to the west and they followed it through hostile native territories. By parlaying with the local tribes they found a way over the Rocky Mountains and to the head of the Snake River which eventually joined the Columbia River and on out to the Pacific. This journey, of around fifteen hundred miles, took almost two years to complete and then they had to send someone back all the way to Saint Louis to break the news of their discovery. This deed has inspired me for years and it was nice to finally witness the only tangible piece of evidence existing from this venture. From there we drove down to Cannon Beach to see the famous Haystack Rock looming out of the Pacific Ocean. This brought up memories of Ilsa Craig Rock rising out of the Irish Sea on Scotland's west coast. After this we drove south down the coast road and stayed the night at a motel in Manzanita with the Pacific Ocean literally pounding the beach directly in full sight from our room. That area is about as opposite as it can be to the Florida landscape but it is wildly beautiful and a visit that I will never forget. They have rain forests up there which are so green and fertile that you could easily hide an army of men just by walking about a hundred yards off any given road or path. The trees are so tall and straight that they seem to reach way up to the skies. If it wasn't for the consistent rain this would be a place that I could seriously relocate to. People are much more rural in these parts and the pace of living almost grinds to a complete stand still. Just south of here is where I lost my harp in Sam Frank's Disco.

Both of my wife's daughters live at Marathon which is in the Florida Keys almost exactly halfway between Miami and Key West. Danielle, the older of the two girls, and her husband Lee are both sheriffs with Monroe County which encompasses all of The Keys. The younger daughter Michelle, who has two daughters Brooke and Cailey, invited her mom and me to have a long weekend stay at the exclusive resort where she had recently hired in. The resort is called Hawk's Cay and virtually takes up almost all of the island known as Duck Key. Michelle wanted to work as a waitress because the tips were said to be good but to her chagrin, she was put to work the front desk. The money there was not that great but she did get to see all the famous people because they always had to check in at the front desk to get their room or chalet assignment. We could only afford to stay at this amazing place by getting Michelle's company discount which dropped the price down to a third of what it would normally be. We stayed in the main hotel of the resort but around the fifty-acre island perimeter were chalets where the rich and famous stayed with there families and away from the madding crowds. The resort has its own private beach, an outdoor dolphin pool and loads of events that the children could be signed up for, to enable the parents time to relax, and a huge catamaran that you could take a two hour cruise on. While we were there Michelle told us that some very famous people were also booked in. Brad Pitt and his family were there, George Hamilton was there filming a television commercial and Keith Richards, of the Rolling Stones, was also relaxing and basking in the sun. This must have been more enjoyable than his usual past time of falling out of coconut trees. Of course, these super stars were hidden away in a secluded area where the security was extremely rigid and not seen by any of us regular guests. Michelle also had to give a tour to the security staff of ex-president Jimmy Carter who was arriving there the week after our visit. This, she said, was an extremely thorough and exhausting job as they had to check every minute detail to ensure that the security aspect of the resort left out nothing that must be desired for a VIP's safety. All this fame and intrigue added to the charisma of the whole visit and after the long sunny day's end we would gather around an open pit fire and discuss that day's pleasures with some of the other guests. As is our normal penchant, when visiting any of The Keys, we drove down to Key West to raise a drink to the late Captain Tony at his bar of the same name. We also had a few toddies for our bodies at the Green Parrot where their motto is that you are welcome but no snivelling is allowed. You just have to love The Keys with their piratical tendencies and veiled threats that all mutinous dogs shall be forced to walk the plank and be dropped into the ocean like a rock.

Lyn in a cheeky mood

Sharon, Richard "Piano Man" Harris and Pete Morrell

Who is this guy?

A Scottish lass with Lyn and Sharon

Seven

Living With Nature

Almost every morning, if you are looking for me, you only have to check out the café on the beach about one hundred and fifty yards from my house. It is aptly name the Gulfside Café and I can be found sitting there reading the morning newspaper and having a cup of coffee. Since I have lived here for the past twelve years this has been my modus operandi. Probably because of the hot climate, I rarely eat when I first wake up. I need about an hour before the taste buds liven up and send messages to my brain that it is time for breakfast. My wife has told me that, when I finally go to meet our maker, she will ask our friends and owners to erect a plaque and affix it above the two top table, out on the back patio, where I usually sit. It is a wonderful way to start the day while over looking the peerless blue Gulf of Mexico. About one thousand miles straight across we are approximately level with the Rio Grande and the Texas/Mexico border. I am told that this vast expanse of water has the most variety of fish second only to the Great Barrier Reef in the Coral Sea off the shores of Australia. I can sit there in the morning and watch Bottle-Nosed Dolphins and the occasional Manatee frolicking in the water. At certain times of the year I can watch large tarpon rise to the surface, roll and plunge to the depths of the ocean. I can watch pelicans and ospreys dive out of the clear blue sky, from great heights, into the water to catch fish. On the shoreline I can watch white and grey herons, egrets, skimmers, terns, curlews and various species of gulls as they go about there daily routine of searching for morsels to eat. This nature abounds all around me while I am being pampered by some fresh-faced young waitress who ensures that my cup of coffee is never empty until I am done. Around me excited tourists marvel at the nearness of all this wildlife which most locals are so used to seeing that they almost take it for granted. I have never felt so close to nature and I have never experienced such a multitude of so many wonderful natural sights. In my own front yard I invariably see mocking birds, spoonbills, parrots and doves nesting in the many trees and bushes that I have planted since arriving here. Working in my yards with potted and in-ground plants is a constant joy. Of course, between the months of May and November I can only work in the yard before 10:00 AM and after 6:00 PM as the temperature hovers consistently between ninety and one hundred degrees Fahrenheit. Never-the-less working in my garden gives me such a sense of achievement and, lets face it, with high temperatures and a good supply of heavy rain, during the summer, I need to do very little except sit back and watch nature perform its miracles.

Because we are so much nearer to the equator, than most parts of America, when it does rain the heavens open up and it absolutely pours down. As we used to say in the Old Country it rains cats and dogs. Here in Florida we have more lightning in one storm, than most places have in a year. In Florida, the Highway 4 corridor between Tampa through Orlando and over to Daytona is known as Lightning Alley. Now lightning can be deadly dangerous and it is said that it can be as hot as the surface of the sun. It has frequently taken lives and is the main instigator of wildfires which burn up thousands of acres of forest each year. Personally, I love thunderstorms and will often go out and stand on my front porch and watch these violent displays. I will even stand out in the warm rain and get a good soaking but I never stand under trees and I never walk around carrying anything that resembles a lightning rod. The famous golfer Lee Trevino is the only man that I have heard of that has been struck by lightning twice and survived. Of course the metal golf club which he was wielding above his head during the storms is the obvious reason that he was signalled out for such severe treatment. One of my all time most amazing sights that I have ever seen was when flying from Atlanta, Georgia to Tampa, Florida at night. It was pitch black as we flew over the top of the clouds during a thunder storm and watching the heavens light up in a colossal display of awesome power was breath taking. Sitting there in the comfort of my seat, at thirty two thousand feet, I was able to look down on top of this massive spectacle of raw energy and power. It was just as if some almighty being was pulling a huge electrical switch on and off at will. This incident remains indelibly imprinted in my minds eye and is something that I will never forget. It makes one realize just how powerful nature can be and how insignificant we humans are in the greater scheme of things. When you consider earthquakes, volcanoes, tsunamis, hurricanes, tornadoes and the likes, it is a wonder that the human race has survived thus far. Yet we human beings, having survival as one of our primary instincts, can rise from the ashes of despair and start all over again, virtually with nothing, and make a complete recovery. What a buttocks clenching thought this subject provokes.

A few months ago my daughter Louise and my grandson Jack came over from England for a short vacation. We had a wonderful time together particularly since Jack is now of the

adventurous age. He wanted to see some alligators [croco-
dile impersonators] in the wild and to this end we all went
for a day out to the Myakka State Park, which is just off I-75
near the Venice exit. We all took one of the Park's magic boat
rides on the lake and did see a good amount of alligators as
this is their natural habitat. When the boat arrived at the far
side of the lake our tour guide spotted a bald eagle perched
up at the top of a huge tree. As the guide steered the boat
closer it became evident that there was, in fact, a family of
four of these amazing birds there. I have seen an occasional
bald eagle, usually in flight, but I had never before seen so
many in one spot and up so close. The guide drifted the boat
over, as near as he possibly could, so that all the passengers
had a photo opportunity. Up close like this you can gauge the
full size of these majestic creatures and it is no wonder that
this bird was chosen as the national symbol of America. The
Native American Indians revere this iconic bird and often
wear its feathers in their head dresses, However, the feathers were collected from dead bald eagles as it was thought
that to kill one was a villainous act that would bring nothing
but bad luck upon the perpetrator. These birds are making a
comeback after their numbers were decimated by the use of
DDT as a crop spray. Since this invasive chemical has now
been banned from use on farm lands the bald eagle population is growing and becoming healthier. Jack was delighted
with this turn of events and he now had yet another amazing story that he can tell his pals back in England. Florida is
one of the few States of America where it is quite common to
witness the bald eagle in the wild.

Another story concerning the realm of nature happened
several years ago when I hosted three young Welsh rugby
players at my home here on Anna Maria Island. Visitors
to these parts should always air on the cautious side while
tramping about in the wild because, being a semi-tropical

land, we do have some creatures and plants that will bite, sting or stick you. Now I don't want to scare the pants off people but there are certain things that they must be aware of for their own well being. For instance, I always tell my visitors never to touch or try to pick up any snake that they might come across, no matter how innocuous it might appear. We have many species of snakes and some look almost exactly alike but their demeanors are completely different. Here in my yard I will sometimes see a black racer which is harmless but there is another snake that resembles a baby black racer but is in fact a pigmy rattler. The racer is harmless so long as it is not provoked but the pigmy, being a viper, will bite you and it is poisonous albeit not deadly. Another thing I always tell my visitors is never to swim in the ocean after dark because this is the time when sharks feed. The rule always quoted by Floridian born people is you can swim from five to nine not from nine to five. This is a generality and more accurately it should be said not to swim after sundown or before sun up. Unbeknownst to me one of the three Welsh boys, Harry, would slip out of the house and take an early morning beach run. Then to cool off he would take a nice, leisurely swim in the Gulf of Mexico as the sun was barely rising. One morning, while taking his morning dip, he noticed a man walking the beach and when he came level with Harry, he stopped dead in his tracks and seemed riveted at the unfolding scene. When Harry finally emerged from the ocean the curious onlooker told him that all the time he was swimming there was a shark cruising back and forth in the water, about twenty yards further out behind him. The thought of being shark bait gave Harry the chills and he immediately ceased his early morning activities.

I have spoken to people who have been two hundred feet in the air while paragliding and they have seen six foot sharks swimming right past people in the water and the people have been totally unaware. I don't want it to sound like this is a dangerous place to live but usually when you hear of a bad person versus animal story, it is usually because the person has let his guard down or had a lapse of common sense. Two people, that I personally know, have been stung in the ocean by sting rays and they have told me that it is one of the most painful experiences of their lives. During the summer months, when the sting rays are breeding, people are told to shuffle their feet when walking in the water as this prevents a person from stepping on a ray. These rays lie almost completely buried under the sand and it is the stepping on them that triggers the tail to automatically lunge up with its spiky barb. Invariably the barb hit's the person in the lower leg or ankle and is a most unpleasantly painful experience. I have witnessed grown men cry, after such an unfortunate encounter, and the whole situation can be summed up as distraction equaling destruction. Just a few weeks ago I saw on the local TV that a visitor from Michigan was in a canoe with his son fishing when he dropped something in the lake. This guy put his head in the water to try and see the object and in that instant an immature alligator had the man's head in its mouth. The man survived but to the alligator it must have looked like bobbing for apples.

The other evening I finally witnessed the Holy Grail of all nature sights. Everyone living here on this barrier reef island yearns to see one particular event. After living here for the past twelve years I am now amongst a select group of people who have been fortunate enough to be on the beach, at night, when a loggerhead turtle has come in to lay its eggs. It was a Wednesday evening right after we had played soccer and, as is our habit, myself and two of my buddies were sitting at a picnic table having a few cold ones. It was a beautiful, moonlit night, pleasantly warm but not too hot, the sun had set and we were sitting there in the evening darkness. Rico, Oliver and myself were dissecting that evening's soccer game, when we noticed what appeared to be a large mound in the sand. As we looked closer the mound, which was the size of a coffee table, was slowly moving closer to the sand dunes. We walked from the picnic table over to the edge of the dunes and there it was, our first sighting of a unique event. The turtle began to dig a pit in which to deposit her eggs but even though we stood there in silence our presence might have spooked her because she then laboriously crawled away to another location further along the beach. We did not follow her because the least little intrusion on our part could send her scurrying back into the ocean and abort the egg laying process. I stood there and watched for another thirty minutes but she seemed uncertain as to whether or not she was comfortable and so I went home as it was now around 11:00 PM. The following day I went back to see if she had laid but there was no taped off area where I had last seen her which would have indicated a nest. I can only hope that she deposited her eggs, at another sight and returned to her home, the Gulf of Mexico. I can only wish her "bon voyage." I can now cross this event from my bucket list and I have to say, even as I sit here writing about it, I am as excited as a child in a candy store. Life basically boils down to being a series of special events which we glean and keep in our memory banks. As we become older these memorable occasions come to mind and gives us a charge which allows us to keep going forward until the next special event takes place. The more of these events that a person witnesses the richer that person's life becomes. My life is rich because I have travelled far and wide and this is why I express the opinion for others to do the same. Not only do you see wonderful sights but you also meet amazingly interesting people from all walks of life.

Another recent disturbing phenomenon has raised its ugly head and caught the attention of the Fish and Wild Life

Department here in southern Florida. This is the ridiculous trend, which some pet owners have adopted, of releasing their too big to care for pythons into the wild. This is absolutely asinine because these foreign predators have no natural enemies in the Everglades and the conditions are perfect for their survival. They somehow find each other and breed profusely and are infesting our natural habitat. The local animal, bird and even the reptile population is under attack and they have been known to try to feed on alligators as big as six foot long. A Wild Life Ranger was recently flying over the Everglades when he saw a sight on the ground and he could not believe what he thought that he was seeing. He landed the helicopter and walked over to an area where a huge python had tried to swallow a mature gator. The python had in fact exploded with the gator in its mouth and so you had two animals locked together, head to head, and their combined length of the pair was around forty feet. No-one had ever witnessed such a sight in the history of the great state of Florida. This unusual turn of events alerted the Fish and Wildlife as to just how serious the python problem had become. My daughter-in-law Danielle was travelling from our house back home to The Keys one night. She was travelling along Old Highway 41 when in her headlights up ahead she saw a python crossing the road. It was as long as the two-lane road that she was driving along. She stopped and let it make its way across rather than risk ending up in a ditch, at the side of the road, with a really ticked off python. For the Mikasookie Indians who live in the Everglades this is a new dangerous set of circumstances that they have to contend with. They have lived with jaguars, alligators and rattlesnakes for years and are accustomed to their ways but with pythons on the prowl their children and pets are no longer free of danger. Now in Florida there is a specific month of the year specially set aside for the hunting of pythons and the hunters can catch and kill as many as they possibly can. The swamps of southern Florida will not be completely safe until these monster snakes are eradicated. If the owners of these constrictors can be traced from the snakes identification chip they should be severely fined or jailed. Perhaps then they will donate their pets to a zoo instead of dumping their problem on other unsuspecting people.

Just the other day I was walking back to my house, from the Gulfside Café, where I had been having my regular morning cup of coffee. I was cutting through the parking lot which is located beneath the Summer Sands Condominiums. It is quite dark under there and, as good luck would have it, I was not wearing sun glasses because if I was I could have very likely have stepped on a snake. At first I thought that it was a rattlesnake but not having heard the rattled warning and with it not coiling up into a strike mode I thankfully realized that it was not. Although the snake's skin markings were almost identical to a rattler I realized that it was a four foot long rat snake which is indigenous to these parts. This snake is a constrictor but only grows to a maximum of about six foot long and is not in the family of foreign pythons that I spoke about earlier. These types of snakes help to keep nature in balance by getting rid of varmints that are of no use to man nor beast. I watched this ally of ours for a while as he slowly wended on his way and I did not feel threatened at all. The saying that "The only good snake is a dead snake" does not ring true to me. While on the subject of unpleasant surprises, we also have a few nasty spiders down here that you would prefer not to come across. Although the Black Widow is the most well known of its species, it is the Brown Recluse which has the worse bite because the flesh, directly around its bite, will die. These spiders do not seek out people to bite but if a person accidentally comes in contact with one and gets bitten, they will be left with an ugly sort of hollowed looking black scar.

Eight

Strange But True

In the past sixth months my wife has had two almost unexplainable circumstances happen to her concerning the novels that she has written. In the first incident Sharon was talking to one of her high school class mates who she had lost touch with many years ago. I guess her girl friend, who still lives in Michigan and on learning that Sharon was now an author, decided to do a computer search and discovered that she was now living down here in Florida. They began to e-mail each other and Sharon told the friend that her books were available on Amazon. A month or two later the girl friend phoned Sharon to say that she had obtained her novel from Amazon and that she thoroughly enjoyed it. There was only one thing that she found unusual and that was the book was personally signed by Sharon to a lady named Ruth. Sharon was dumbfounded because Ruth is a friend of hers in Florida and it appeared that two personal friends of her had now possessed the very same book. The answer to this riddle was that Ruth had turned her copy of Sharon's book back to Amazon to be used as a credit against a future purchase. The Michigan friend had then ordered the book from Amazon not knowing that they actually resold used books. That in itself is not that unusual but for the same actual book to be owned by two friends, twelve hundred miles apart, is extremely unusual. I am a betting man and the odds of that happening is phenomenal.

The second story concerning one of Sharon's novels happened one day as I was tidying up our backyard patio, where our rear fence backs onto the Queen's Gate Motel. As a matter of fact the last of the motel's bungalows is around ten yards away from our backdoor. As I glanced over, in that direction, there was a man sitting at an outside table and he was reading one of Sharon's books. When I later went back inside our house I said to Sharon that I had noticed that she had sold one of her books to one of the Queen's Gate guests. She said the she did no such thing to which I returned to the back patio and politely asked the man where he got the book from. He told me that he had been loaned the book by another lady guest at the motel and he pointed this person out to me. I again politely posed the same question to her and her answer was quite unusual. On her visit to Anna Maria she was in need of a kitchen table and so she purchased one from a local resale store. It wasn't until she got the table home that she had the presence of mind to open the table drawer and there, inside, was the copy of Sharon's book. The previous owner of the kitchen table was a friend of ours named Tanya and she had inadvertently left the novel in the table drawer. Some people are great believers in the theory that there are certain times when a specific item must be passed on for someone else to benefit from owning it. On occasions this sort of thing naturally happens and instead of bemoaning the item's loss it is considered better to be happy in the anticipation that a good thing has occurred and that pleasure will be gained by the new recipient. This is Sharon's whole attitude concerning these two events as for some reason she feels that this was meant to happen. Sharon is so lucky because, amongst her many assets, she has beautiful skin which gives her the appearance of being a younger woman. I have always said to her, partly in jest, that because of her skin she is probably part American Indian which she has always rejected. Her father unfortunately passed away this past Spring and when she returned from his funeral she brought back some papers concerning her family's history. Sure enough, there it was in black and white. Her grandmother, on her father's side, was born on a Cherokee reservation and if that doesn't make Sharon one quarter Native American Indian then I'll eat my hat. As a sidebar, I once met a Cherokee Chief and he said "How" and so I said " How " back to him. After several minutes of "How," back and forth, he said to me "I didn't know that you could speak Cherokee." To which I replied "It's easy when you know how."

On my most recent visit back to the Wirral area of Cheshire I had two equally jaw dropping events. I was staying at the Bridge Inn Hotel in Port Sunlight and on the Sunday morning I phoned my daughter, Louise, to see what time she, her son Jack and my son Richard would be meeting me to go to the city of Chester for the afternoon. She told me that they were running late and would not be able to meet me until around 3:00 PM. Now they were all staying at my ex-wife's home out in Caldy which just so happens to be about a half of a mile from where there was to be a seven-a-side rugby tournament which, incidentally, I had played in almost forty years earlier. I told her that I would catch a taxi over to Caldy and watch the rugby for three hours and then they could pick me up there. It was a blustery day with scattered showers and I was trying to stay dry and yet still attempted to watch as many games as possible. One game had just finished and so, with a nice hot cup of coffee in hand, I strolled over to the next field to watch another match. I pulled up to the sideline right next to two other gentlemen and I asked what the score was, as I had missed the kick-off. The guy to my immediate left answered me but the second guy almost looked like he had seen a ghost. After a few more minutes of idle conversation the second guy asked if I worked at a café in Florida to which I said that I did. The man was absolutely stunned and told me that he had met me at the café the previous Summer and I had told him that I usually came over to the United Kingdom almost every year. In spite of this he still had never dreamed that we would ever meet and especially not on a wet and dreary day at the side of a rugby field. Well wonders never cease and it probably will not be the last time that this sort of strange encounter will happen to me again. Things like this have been happening throughout my life.

For instance on the very same trip whilst staying at the very same place yet another strange event occurred. It was on the day before the previous story and my family and I were looking around historic Port Sunlight Village. We went to the museum, the Heritage Center and the art gallery. On the way back to the hotel we decided to take a look at the beautiful village church. We were walking along the path that ran around the church and at the back of it was the protruding walls of the inside nave. As we reached that point my family carried on along the regular path but for some unknown reason I veered off down a tiny little path parallel to the nave. When I reached the end of that little path I looked down and there, leaning against the church wall was a commemorative urn with the name Tony Griffiths on it. I stood there stunned because Tony was the scrum-half at Port Sunlight rugby club when I was the outside-half. We were like two peas in a pod back then and I had no idea that his remains were at that church. After I left for America Tony was transferred, with his job, down to the Bristol area and I heard some years later that he had passed away. I guess that I assumed that his remains were somewhere down in that area. None of my rugby buddies knew where Tony was put to rest and here I was standing at the very spot. So that his family would know that I was there, I took out one of my business cards and wrote "Tony, the best scrum-half I ever played with. You will be dearly missed. Taffy. " I hope that the next time his family goes to put flowers in his urn they will find my note and know that someone, from thirty five years ago and four thousand miles away, still cares. I passed on the whereabouts of his remains to a good friend of mine, Joe Byrne, who played with both Tony and I, and he in turn will inform the other members of that once brilliant team.

On a similar visit to that area about four years earlier I was staying at the seaside town of West Kirby and was, one day, shopping on the high street. Inside one of the shops was a notice board festooned with various business cards advertising a myriad of different people and their businesses. One card in particular caught my eye as it was advertising a collector of famous autographs. This peeked my interest as I was in the possession of a good number of these and, wondering what his interest in them was, I took his card from the board and put it in my wallet. I returned to Florida and some two years later I was searching for some information and up popped this business card. On the spur of the moment I decided to telephone the person to see what he actually did. When the gentleman in Wallasea answered the phone he was amazed at the fact that, on a whim, I had decided to phone him from four thousand miles away. He kept interjecting by asking me if this was a prank call and which one of his lunatic friends had set him up. After about the fifth time of his asking I finally persuaded him that he was not being pranked and that this was a genuine call. Apparently he worked in conjunction with a charity and he collected autographs of famous people which would then be auctioned off at various benefit dinners. All monies raised would then go to a specific cause, one of which was the Liverpool Children's Hospital. We discussed the fact that I had the autographs of some very famous people but he was looking for donations and I was looking to sell. Never-the-less I sent him my first book, which in part detailed some stories concerning how I was able to get these autographs, and he in turn sent me a CD of the 1966 England World Cup Soccer Final signed by three of the players from that historic team. If there is one thing that I have learned, by coming to America, it is that sitting on the fence wondering about an event or situation is not an option. If I have a query and I simply need to know the details, I now take immediate action to solve the problem instead of pondering for an insufferable period of time on the issue. I think sometimes in Britain we confuse directness with bad manners and waiting to be told with politeness. I have noticed that because of this, British children tend to be more polite where as American children are less controlled which makes them more outgoing and adventurous. The never say die attitude of American children is what, in my opinion, makes them so good at sports in later life whereas British children tend to be somewhat more cerebral.

Because I have spent half of my life in Britain and the other half in America, I would like to consider myself as having the best of both worlds. I was educated in the UK which gives me a good grasp of the English language, history and geography which puts me at a distinct advantage in these areas. However, coming to the USA has taught me to take calculated risks in business and life in general. I remember that once I had a girlfriend who had to be rushed into hospital with a severe gall stone attack and from what she told me it was a worse pain than child bearing. I went to see her during the normal visiting hours and then went to a bar, just down the street, for some dinner and a few cocktails. I got into some conversations with various people and before I knew it was closing time. On an impulse I decided that I would go back to the hospital to tell her goodnight. I stealthily made my way past all the security personnel and she was delighted to see me as it was a totally unexpected thing for anyone to do. It had been a long day and I was feeling tired and so I climbed onto the bed, on top of the sheets, and fell fast asleep while holding her in my arms. Early the next morning the nurses, upon doing their rounds found us still asleep and locked together. They thought that it was the cutest thing that they had ever seen. Nevertheless, they had to ask me to quickly leave so that they would not get into trouble, with their superiors, for allowing me to slip by them on their watch. I dispatched myself with gratitude and great haste. The point that I am trying to make is that this was the American influence coming out in me because back in Britain I would never have considered such an audacious ruse. I have now developed the capacity to embrace life to the maximum and leave no stone unturned when it comes to seeking out enjoyment and living life to the fullest. A famous song once described this lifestyle as "skipping over the ocean like a stone."

Nine

Into Life a Little Rain Must Fall

I have related many times with regards to what a wonderful life that I now have in the United States but every once in a while someone just has to throw a wrench in the works. Some years ago my wife and I took a trip to that eighth wonder of the world, Las Vegas. If you ever saw the film *Bugsy* you will know that this city was built, straight out off the unyielding desert, because of the complete foresight of a gangster named Bugsy Seigel. At that time, everybody thought he was crazy but he was a visionary because he could envision the endless possibilities for success where everyone else saw failure. His dream cost him his life but what he created will stand as a monument to him forever. He did not go quietly into that dark night and he will be remembered, because of his dream, for an eternity. So, here I am one night playing a slot machine at the Stratosphere when my wife and her brother, who had flown in from Michigan to join us, announced that they wanted to go over to Caesar's Palace Casino. I declined to go with them because I was on a hot run and wanted to ride out my lucky streak. As it happened two hours later my streak had ended and all monies previously won had now gone back to the house. A few hours later my wife and her brother returned bristling with excitement. They took me to one side and explained to me that right outside of the Palace a man appeared from nowhere and asked them if they would be interested in buying a ring which had a gold band and what looked like a one-carat diamond mounted on it. The price tag on this ring was around two thousand dollars and this guy was asking one thousand for it. They walked away on three occasions but the guy kept coming back and lowering his price until finally he settled for two hundred dollars. To all extent of purposes they had done a magnificent job of bartering this street wise guy, down to an amazingly low price and they strutted around like a pair of peacocks. They spent most of that night laughing like hyenas and giving each other high fives. The following week, back in Florida, my wife decided to have the ring appraised by a local jeweller. You can imagine her deflated emotions when she found out that the ring was, in fact, nothing but brass and glass. At the most it was probably worth about twenty dollars and when my wife shared these facts on the phone with her brother, you could almost hear his anguish from Michigan all the way down to Florida. Of course this amused my offbeat sense of humor and I didn't miss any opportunity to rub their noses in their mire of misfortune for many years since that fateful day. In Vegas, it is not just the case of walking the walk and talking the talk, you actually have to be on your guard at all times because Vegas has attracted the best con-men in the business. The old saying of "All that glitters is not gold" can certainly apply here and remember what happens in Vegas stays in Vegas. In other words the police turn a blind eye to these petty crimes because they have bigger fish to fry. That is a strange analogy when it is considered that we are talking about a city smack dab in the middle of the Nevada desert.

Another incident happened when Sharon and I went to a book signing in Alexandria, Virginia. The book signing itself was in an expensive Hilton Hotel just across the Potomac River from the country's capitol of Washington D.C. The trip, on the whole, was entirely successful except for one bizarre incident. We had booked into a less expensive motel a few miles away from the Hilton and drove to and from there in our car which we had driven up all the way from Florida. The motel appeared to be half empty as they were in the middle of renovating the place. They put us in a room on the third floor, which we didn't mind until we found out that we were up there all on our own. The room next to ours had the curtains wide open and we could plainly see that it was being used as a temporary store room because it was full of furniture. That night, when we returned from the Hilton, we had an eerie feeling as we entered our room and felt that we were being watched. Because of this I not only locked the door but I put the latch chain on and jammed a chair back under the door handle. Well it was a good thing that I did because in the middle of the night someone tried to kick our door open. The lock broke and the door flew open but fortunately the chain and chair held. Sharon let out a scream that would have awoken the dead and we heard the footsteps of two people running away. We were both very relieved that we had prevented someone from robbing or, God forbid, killing us. We tried to comfort ourselves by saying that perhaps they were trying to steal furniture but got the wrong room. This was no help and we basically sat up for the rest of the night as neither of us could sleep. The next morning I complained to a young African-American lady in charge of the front desk but she didn't seem to grasp the importance of the whole situation. Since we only had one night left of our stay we decided just to change rooms to be nearer the main guest population and the swimming pool. Why we could not have been put there in the first place beats the hell out of me. I guess that we almost danced with the devil that night.

I have lived on Anna Maria Island for the past twelve years and although I have heard about a number of shark bites, I had never heard of a full blown shark attack. Well, all that radically changed just recently when a bull shark arbitrarily decided to take a chunk out of a young man's thigh. This unlucky young man and five of his good friends opted for a leisurely day out with a boat trip to an area five miles west of the Island. It was a beautiful sunny day and the three couples planned to languish in the ocean by swimming and floating off their well appointed boat. After a while the three restless young men decided to try their hand at spear fishing because they were anchored on top of a deep channel where a good variety of the bigger fish are known to linger. They suited up and entered the deep, dark blue abyss and immediately began to hunt their prey. However, where there is game fish there is undoubtedly sharks lurking in the same vicinity. These intrepid predators, like the young men, are also seeking big fish and to snag any tasty morsel that might come their way. The shark is, without a doubt, much more skilled at achieving this goal. The young men had not been in the water for very long before their activity was detected by one of the most dangerous of all this savage species, the ominous bull shark.

Spear fishing is a highly dangerous pastime because when fish are speared they thrash about on the end of the spear and, more importantly, they bleed. These are the very symptoms that will alert a shark from around a mile away that a fish is in distress and they will immediately come to investigate the circumstance. This is a very good reason why ladies, during their menstrual cycle, should stay at the swimming pool and not go into the ocean during this time. In fact, when braver people actually fish for shark they use this to their advantage and deliberately bait the ocean with bleeding fish to attract the shark, a practice known as "chumming the waters." The shark will inevitably follow the scent of blood right to its very source and proceed to devour whatever it finds. One of the young men had in fact speared a nice-sized fish and had come to the surface of the water to hand off the catch to his friends on board. While he was treading water and talking to his ship mates a dark torpedo came rocketing up from the depths below and viciously bit him. The eight foot long mature bull shark mistakenly identified him as the dying fish but showed no mercy. It tore into the young man's left thigh but the swimmer fought back punching his assailant hard on the nose and the shark temporarily let go. As he screamed for help there immerged a five foot circle of blood surrounding the young man in the water and on seeing this the others, on the boat, quickly hauled him aboard. They applied a tourniquet, put out a radio alert signal and headed for the nearest site where a medical rescue helicopter could be landed. Their prompt action, without a doubt, saved this young man's life as it was found out later that he had already lost four pints of blood and the human body can only hold nine pints at its optimum capacity. His friends delivered him, in record time, to the Rod and Reel Pier at the north end of the Island and the Emergency Technicians took him to a major local hospital. There it took around eight hundred sutures to sew back into position the large flap of flesh which hung from his leg. The gaping wound was so deep that it went right down to the young man's thigh bone which was clearly visible. Any lightly built person, such as myself, with less meat on his thigh would have definitely had that leg taken clean off. If the young man would have been further away from the boat or if the shark had come back for a second attack, he would not be alive today to tell the tale. Lady Luck had intervened and preserved this most fortunate of beings.

I was on the beach one day when a passing tourist casually asked me if I thought that there were sharks out there in the ocean. I emphatically told him that the ocean was the shark's domain and that they were always out there at any given time. We, the humans, are the aliens of the seas and we should never forget this when we enter their waters. The attack on this young man occurred in broad daylight and belies the theory that sharks only feed, or as we say attack, at night. Anyone who enters the Gulf of Mexico waters must be fully aware that they are sharing the ocean with a creature which has survived and evolved for thousands of years. At no time should vigilance ever be discarded because with this expert hunter and killer in the water the consequences could prove fatal. Self preservation must be the prime concern when entering these vast waters and no lapse in concentration can be tolerated. For instance, not too long ago another man was bitten by a shark, albeit not severely, because he emptied his bucket of bait fish into the sea while he was still standing in the water. This is akin to a hunter shooting himself in the foot which is just about as dumb of an occurrence that could possibly transpire under duress. I rest my case on this issue. As a foot note, one of the young ladies that happened to be on the boat that day was named Oceania. Perhaps then it was not Lady Luck at all but the timely action of Neptune, himself, that saved the day. Wonders never cease!

Although I have given the average angler a bad rap I must conversely point out that fishing, as a sport or commercial venture, is big business down here in the semi-tropical waters of Florida. This category of fishing is a horse of another color because these people, unlike the weekend fishermen, are out to catch the biggest and rarest fish they can find and the Gulf of Mexico is the place to find them. For sport fishing you have to hire a charter boat and a captain who knows these waters like the back of his hand. The boat must have a depth finder that can locate the shoals of fish and the boat must also have the heavy duty rod and reels to bring those babies in once they are hooked. We are talking huge fish like all the varieties of sharks, tarpon, marling, sword fish, cobia, red snapper and grouper which are basically called trophy fish. The bait fish used by these fishermen are often Spanish mackerel and these, by any other standard, would be prized enough as keepers to take home and eat. For these types of extra large fish, and I mean whoppers, the boat has to go as much as twenty miles off shore and stay out there from sun up to sun down. To do this will cost a good amount of money to hire the boat and usually four or five people will group together and share this cost. However, when they begin to cast it as every man for himself because the biggest fish earns the biggest bragging rights for that day. This basically means that a person is competing against everyone else on the boat and that is when it becomes a sport. Commercial fishing in these parts is operated out of the small neighboring town of Cortez and these trawlers go out for up to three weeks at a time or until they fill the salt water hold. This is extremely hard work and some of the Cortez families have been doing this for generations and it is in their blood. These fishermen are paid on a percentage of the total catch and so the more fish, that they bring in, the more money they will earn. On the boat while they are fishing it is all work but when these fishermen arrive back in port they spend money as if it were going out of fashion. You might have heard the expression of a person "Spending money like a drunken sailor," well it is true. When these guys are paid and hit town I have seen bar bills as high as five hundred dollars because they seem to buy anyone and everyone a drink. Hey, ho and up she rises, early in the morning !

Lyn at Tintagel Castle, Cornwall

Gateway to the probable site of Camelot

Burial site of Celtic Kings

Prehistoric grave of an ancient King at Lanyan Coit, Cornwall

Ten

Toil and Trouble

In the main, life on the paradise island of Anna Maria goes along quite smoothly but once in a while a small amount of trouble will pop up and, in more cases than not, it is caused by over zealous visitors. It is understandable that people flock to this island to get married, to vacation and, in some instances, just to party hardy which can quite often lead to some problems.

One such problem occurred one night when Sharon and I were walking home from the small downtown area of Bradenton Beach. On Bridge Street there are a small group of amusement places, shops and bars which is only about two blocks long but, on the weekends, that is where most of the people on the south end of the island gather. We were coming out of the renowned Drift In and as we were passing The Sports Bar there was a small incident where it appeared that a young man was either refused entrance to that establishment or conversely was being asked to leave. This male individual seemed very intoxicated and as we walked by him I made some passing reference about the man's out of order behavior. We carried on walking home and after a few blocks Sharon noticed that the drunken man was following us at a distance. The further we walked the closer he was getting to us and this began to worry my wife. Sharon was really becoming scared and I told her to be prepared because if this drunk caught up to us I was going to have to deck him. Sure enough not even a hundred yards later he was right at our backs and I just turned and hauled off. My punch was precisely aimed and caught him on his lower jaw in a downward movement. For a second he just stood there but then he reeled forward, from the force of the punch, landing in my arms and dragging me to the ground with him. I told Sharon not to worry because I was still in charge of the situation and that if this guy persisted I would hit him a few more times. The guy, still being on the ground, told me that he did not want to fight and apologized. We both stood up and I explained to him that the only reason I punched him was because his actions were frightening my wife and my job was to protect her. Again he apologized and staggered off into the night and was soon out of sight. The guy was almost exactly my size, about five foot eight and around one hundred and sixty pounds in weight but I could not have him approach us like that when his intentions were not clear. In a case where the safety of you or a loved one is in imminent danger, it is best to act first and ask questions later. You could say that my decisive action rendered me as pleased as Punch.

Another distasteful episode happened one day when I was working in my backyard. Out of nowhere there was a dog next to me. Not only was it a dog, it was a pedigree English Bulldog. I knew that this dog was not owned by any of my neighbors and so I was puzzled as to where it came from. Over the back fence, sitting at the motel, was a young couple and so I asked them if they had lost a dog. The young lady of the duo jumped up and came over to the fence to see the dog and she was immediately enamored with it. She said that it wasn't hers but she would take it up to the front office of the motel to see if it belonged to any of the other guests. I turned the dog over to her and continued about my chores in the yard. About an hour later another young lady, who unbeknownst to me was a renter at the original house directly across the street from me, asked me if I had seen her dog. She described the dog to me and it was the very same beautiful bulldog that was in my yard earlier. I told her what had happened and that the last time I had seen her dog was when the lady guest at the motel said that she was taking it to the front office. The dog owner went there to retrieve her dog but the office clerk told her that there had been no dog brought there. Here in Florida, dog napping is rife as it is a business that can bring in quick and easy money. A pedigree bulldog, I have since learned, can bring in as much as two thousand dollars. These people steal dogs and, after the heat has died down, they advertise and sell them. I was shocked to find out that this was one of those cases. Apparently this couple was from Lakeland, a town about an hour away, and they had put the dog in their van and drove over there, dropped the dog off and drove back as though nothing had occurred. The next day my neighbor, who owned the house opposite me, asked me what had happened and I gave him all the details concerning the couple at the motel. He went to the motel office and got the names and address of that couple and furnished this to the local police. They in turn had the Lakeland police to go to the house and when they were there they could here a dog barking inside but no one answered the door. This has been a real learning experience for me because, up to that date, I did not know that people like this existed. Since this incident I have been told numerous, similar stories and it has become a sad state of affairs when a family's beloved pet can be taken so abruptly. This should be a lesson to us all and this practice not only extends to dogs it also, more importantly, includes our precious children.

Another story in this ignoble category, occurred right out in front of my house one day. It was during the time when the two new houses were being constructed across the street from me. There is inevitable congestion on a building site as various tradesmen park their trucks and different building supplies are dropped off. Quite often I would have to ask someone or other to move their vehicle so that we could enter or leave our driveway. On the whole everybody was pleasant and obliging and although times were difficult, in the most part we all managed to get along. However, there was an exception to this rule and this man was the driver of a huge truck that delivered and removed the massive industrial waste containers. He would block the road completely while he talked to other people or made extensive phone calls. On this particular day I politely asked him how long he would be in the middle of the road. My wife would be home from work soon and he was blocking both my driveway and the auxiliary parking spot that we used when needed. This guy told me in no uncertain words that he would be there for as long as he damn well pleased and that it was none of my darn business, except he didn't say darn. So I said back to him that if I came over to his street and did the same thing in front of his house then, by the same token, I would assume that this would not upset him either. This made this very large African-American truck driver more annoyed and he and I were nose to nose for a while there and the whole scenario took a turn for the worse when he told me that he would mess me up. At this threat of violence I told him that I was going to call the police and as a parting shot I said that I hoped that he didn't have any outstanding warrants or was on probation. This seemed to galvanize his thoughts and he pulled his truck out and left in a hurry.

I told the builder all about this altercation and he said that he would make sure that this particular driver would not make any more trips to the building site on my street. Everybody went about their business and the whole incident drifted into oblivion. That is until around six months later when I bumped into the builder again. There had been a recent event where the police had gone to an address to serve a warrant on a known criminal. The guy refused to surrender and when the arresting officers entered the house a gun fight ensued. The criminal had retreated up into the attic and the two officers tried to go up there after him and he shot both of them dead. The SWAT team was sent for and they shot about a hundred rounds into the attic and, after not hearing anything from the criminal, they took a bull dozer and lifted the roof right off the house. The assassin was found dead in the rubble but it was a bad day for the police who had lost two brave officers. This story was followed, blow by blow, through all the local television channels and the perpetrator's name, Hydra Lacey, was all over the news papers. What the builder had sought me out for was to tell me that the killer was none other than the truck driver that I had argued with in front of my house. I felt a cold shiver go down my spine when I realized that I had confronted such a bad person and that he probably had a hand gun in the glove box of his truck. Being an ex-rugby player the large size of a man does not phase me because I have seen big men hurt and even cry. However, bravery is no substitute for a bullet and my flush of courage must, in future, be curbed. I have been referred to as a man amongst men but even I can see the futility of making my lovely wife into a premature widow.

There is one other thing, down here in the deep south, that visitors should be conscious about and always on guard from it. It is blatantly obvious and yet every year thousands of people forget to take precautions from it and suffer the consequences. I am referring to the sun which rises with almost monotonous regularity in these parts and burns the skin of so many unprepared tourists. Being nearer to the equator, the ultra-violet rays from the sun are much stronger and pene-trates a person's skin more deeply. Most Americans, because of their mixed heritage, have no problems but the Arian/ Celtic/Norse types with their fair hair and light colored eyes could be candidates for sunburn if they do not take the neces-sary precautions. When we are young and our skin is at its best we tend to flaunt the adversity of the sun. However, as we get on in age and our skin becomes less resilient, we white-skinned types must be on guard at all times when face to face with a powerful sun. I had to take one of my house visitors to the hospital with third-degree sunburn after a day on the beach when the sun was hardly showing at all

It is harder for kids to grow up, in this technological age than it was for me back in my time. When I grew up in Wales it was uncommon for families to have phones in their homes. Most of us were too poor for such luxuries and so, in the main, communication was done face to face thus making it crystal clear what was being said and agreed to by both parties. Even when phones in the home became the norm, we could still communicate with someone and by hearing the tone of their voice a reasonable understanding was formed as to what was being said. Now we come to present-day texting and this leaves the sender's position being that they cannot see or hear the other person and so it is now a case of trusting that the other person will answer the text and, at the same time, be truthful. With having no real knowledge, as to what is going on, all they can now do is to wait in hope for a reply. Even if their contact does reply on occasions they only trans-mit the information that they are willing to give. Therefore it takes forever to get all the details needed to achieve anything and sometimes, if need be, information is deliberately omit-ted if that person does not want to be honest. The other day I witnessed a teenaged girl spend almost the whole day texting a boy to hook up with him to go roller skating that night and, after all that effort she never did get a clear reply. If a phone is available and allowed, it should always be used if a prompt and reliable reply is needed. Otherwise a whole day could be wasted on frivolous messages and still the required relevant information may not be forthcoming. Case in point, in Saudi Arabia they will not allow the *Flintstones* to be shown on television but Abba Dahbi do.

In Wales, where I come from, a man's word is everything and once given and it is followed through to the letter. His word is his bond and if a person should go back on his promise he is branded as unreliable and is never completely trusted ever again. From that point on he can never be fully trusted or taken seriously and his worth in his community is for ever diminished. He is hence forth considered to take on the guise of a two-tongued serpent.

Eleven

Revisiting My Youth

One beautiful evening my wife and I were sitting on our lawn chairs at the beach watching the sun set while having a few cocktails when a local island guy rode past on his bicycle. I knew this guy because his son was in the same class at the Island Elementary School as my wife's granddaughter Brooke. Learning that he played soccer up near St. Louis I had persuaded him to play soccer for my Michigan team who came down every winter to play against Sarasota. On seeing me he came back and told me that a bunch of guys gathered at a local field for a kick around game of soccer. He informed me the days and times and invited me along and he said that it was a laid back type of affair with no real competitiveness involved. Now I have always been very athletic and have been in competitive sports for many years. Back in the old country I played rugby for twenty five years in Wales and England. My last game that I played was on the Saturday before I flew out to America on the following Monday. On coming to the USA I began playing soccer which lasted another twenty five years but at this particular point in time I had not kicked a ball or run a step for five years. Most men of my age would not even consider taking up such a vigorous sport again but I had not been happy, for some time, concerning putting on weight and feeling sluggish. It might have been the cocktails or the ambience of the occasion but, whatever it was, I told this young man that I would be there the following week. Well it turned out to be somewhat more serious of a game than he described and for the first month I was walking around as stiff as a toy soldier. After that tortuous month my legs began to loosen up and my lungs began to take in air a little easier and my game has slowly improved to the point where I can now enjoy it. The two things that these games have given me is a fitter body and a great bunch of friends. I am once again mixing with people of a similar mind and determination as my own. This is a unique type of camaraderie that only people who have played at this level can appreciate. Before, I used to have ordinary friends but now I have true confidants. We are a mixed bag from professional people to tradesmen and students and if any of us need help with a problem all we have to do is ask and the appropriate person will step forward. Point in case, the two new houses across the street from me were burglarized and one of our players, Chris, who is in the security alarm business, took it upon himself to put two of his company's product warning signs in my yard even though I do not have a security system. He just felt that this would make my family and I feel more at ease. A remarkably nice and heartfelt gesture.

The Island Rowdies, the name which we have adopted, are a real mixed bag and cover just about every sort of player imaginable. We have men, we have boys, we have girls. We have good players, bad players, very experienced players and those that have never played in an organized team before. We have some that want to learn the game as it should be and we have those that run around like chickens with their heads cut off. We have Americans, Canadians, Mexicans, Greeks, Croatians, Asians, Turkish, Germans, English, Polish and, of course, Welsh. We also have one Canadian, ex-pro player who has been diagnosed with cancer and is currently undergoing chemotherapy. Amazingly, he still puts his boots on and plays with us for as long as his body allows. What a brave person and a true islander. Just the other day we had four young men from Grange Mouth, Scotland, who were over here on holiday, just turn up out of the blue to ask if they could join in a game with us. They had heard from a local islander that there was a crazy gang who met up to play soccer twice a week in ninety degree heat and decided to seek us out. We play without referees because it is cheaper and we divide the players into teams by the color of their shirts. We try to balance the teams by ensuring an equal amount of each age and skill level that seems appropriate. If one team gets too far ahead on goals, the game is stopped and the teams are re-balanced more evenly. We have had several independent people with soccer knowledge come and watch our games and their immediate response is to tell us that we are good enough to play in the local organized soccer leagues. However, we feel that this would take the fun and spontaneity out of the game and the fact that all leagues involve a good deal of travel, for out of town matches, this would make it an unattractive proposition to most of our gang. There are about half a dozen of this bunch who have played league soccer at varying levels and would not want to go down that dusty road again. In those types of situations there is usually a good deal of politics and in fighting with a lot of finger pointing when games are lost. In our current situation a player can turn up when he wants, play for as long as he wants and walk off the field anytime he wants, no questions asked. If a player wants to take a few weeks off to go fishing or to go on vacation, he doesn't have to ask or tell anyone, he just does it. This keeps everything at a low level of maintenance with no reporting to any trainers, managers or captains. In other words it is a typical island kind of disorganization which is played with flair and good sportsmanship which must be applauded and long may it last.

From this rag tag bunch of players grew the first Anna Maria Community Center in-house soccer league which is played on a Thursday evening and does not clash with our previously explained set up. Yes this is a low level league but all the games are played at one location under flood lights if necessary just a few miles up the road from our pitch in Holmes Beach. The league has a rating procedure for all of our players, to make the teams equal, and then they sprinkled in the other players who had little or no game experience. The teams worked out to be very even and most of the games were close and well contested. At the end of the regular games the top four teams moved into the play-offs. There was the two semi-finals followed the next night by the championship game. All of these games were extremely exciting with the crowds of supporters going wild. In the first semi, the Tim Tedesco team beat the Croatian contingent surprisingly easy. In the second semi Josh Sato's team beat my team by four goals to three in a game that went right down to the wire. I have quite often been cavalierly quoted as saying that I would rather lose a good game than win a bad one. Well this was one of those occasions where the actual game was bigger than the end result. Even if we had won through to the Final my team was so depleted with injuries that it is highly unlikely that we could have succeeded. The final was won by the Sato team but with the score lock at one to one it took a penalty shootout to decide the game. The losing team missed just one of their penalties and, in the final analysis, that's all it took. However, Tim's team had a number of good chances to finish the game off in regulation time but just could not convert. Congratulations to the players of all the teams for putting in such a concerted effort. The Most Valuable Player, in the whole tournament, must go to the goal keeper on the Sato team who made save after remarkable save to keep his team in top position. The bravery award must go to the oldest player who, at the age of seventy one, amazed all and sundry. Bravo.

Another unusual soccer incident happened to me when I was at the I.M.G. Complex in Bradenton watching the USA Under 17 Boys team playing their Brazilian counterparts. It was a cooler February day, by Florida standards, and I was wearing a tracksuit top given to me some years earlier by a young Irish boy who played for Madonna College in Michigan. He was visiting me and when he returned North he didn't have a warm jacket to wear and so I gave him a down filled jacket which I had no need for in the South. There was quite a crowd at the game and it would be hard to find anyone if you didn't know exactly where they were. All of a sudden I heard someone shout my name and when I turned around there was Pete Alexander a guy who I used to play with up in Canton, Michigan. He spotted me because of the top that I was wearing and he, if anyone, should recognize it because he used to be the coach of that team. He was glad to see me and asked me where I got the Madonna top from. I told him that Gary Bell had given it to me and he didn't really care because he thought that Gary had taken it back to Ireland. Pete was actually down here on a coaching course and it just happen to coincide with the soccer match that we met at. The World moves in mysterious ways and it is somewhat amazing that one garment could touch so many different lives. Pete invited me to meet him that night at a party given for all the coaches on his course, at a sports bar called Cherries. All the food and drinks were free and Nike watches were given out to all who attended. Of course, it was assumed by everyone in attendance that I was one of the many coaches and I graciously accepted all the gifts that were bestowed upon me with great humility. It is said, here in America, that what goes around comes around. This basically means that an act of kindness is often paid back, somewhere down the road, by a similar act although not necessarily from the same person. This type of weird justice has befallen me on quite a few occasions, some could say too often to be a fluke. Recently a man in Wales bought me a drink and when I asked him what it was for and he answered the last time that he saw me, some ten years earlier, he had admired a shirt that I was wearing. The day I left to return to America I put that shirt on a hanger and put it on the door knob of his front door. He had never forgotten that random act of kindness and after ten long years he had repaid my thoughtfulness. In some ways I could be considered a *menace to sobriety*.

The group of islanders that I play soccer with, as I have said before, is a real mixed bunch. We have school kids, college kids, tradesmen, professionals, unemployed and even some retired people which span the spectrum from around fourteen years of age to the early seventies. Right now I feel a little concerned about the college kids because, unlike things were before the recent recession, it may be that perhaps now it is not as desirable to spend four to eight years in college and then be released into a job market which has rapidly declined. There is such a glut of over qualified people already out there who cannot find work and so what is the point of further flooding the market with a rash of the same-status job seekers. What the country needs is for young people to turn their attention to such jobs as plumbers, auto mechanics, electricians and carpenters because if they cannot find work through the normal channels, working for regular companies, then they can do side jobs on an individual basis. This way they can still pull in some money to keep their families fed during the tough times. Five years ago I had three Welsh rugby players come and stay with me here in Florida. They had just graduated from college and were full of the joys of life. One of them was real lucky to meet and marry a young American girl and his father-in-law set him up as a trainer at a gymnasium that the family owned. The other two took the conventional path and could only get work as part-time teachers until around four years later when some older teacher retired and gave them their full time opportunity. Companies now have such an amount of over-qualified candidates that they can pick and chose who they want and pay them half the wage that they would have been worth five years ago. That is what is known as a buyers market and the present day college graduate is thankful just to get that pittance.

Back in the mid 1950s I took a five year apprenticeship instead of going to college right out of school. Perhaps we have to bring something like this back because when times are bad it is not so much what you earn as what you don't spend. This way if you are a tradesman you can fix your own household problems and not have to pay someone else to do it for you. Some people might find these views a bit radical but times, they are a-changing and we must look at our economic problems in a different light. A thirty year old man once told me that he would not work at a job for ten dollars an hour. I told him that he was a fool because it was not the ten dollars that was the most important fact. It is the fact that he was out there meeting people and networking with them. The other point that he hadn't considered, was that by staying at home he was increasing all his household bills like electricity, food and talking on the phone. I told him that there was work in the oil fields of Alaska and in the building industry in Texas but he answered that he would not consider moving. I had to remind him that America was built on people moving from Europe, some of them travelled anywhere from three to six thousand miles away, to start life all over again hoping for the chance to better their lives. This man has now moved about three hundred miles away and is working for a few bucks more than ten dollars an hour. Some people just think "arse backwards" and need the proverbial kick up the back-side to become motivated.

The fact that I can play soccer, or even run at my tender age, is because of a piece of advice which was given to me when I was about eleven years of age. I had started to play rugby at Abersychan Tech school and the Sports Master there, Rodney Williams, taught me to never get caught in a tackle with both feet on the ground. The end result of this is that, although I have had quite a few injuries in my time, I have never damaged my knees and without good knees a person cannot run. My undamaged knees have kept me active in competitive sports for around sixty years and if that is not a testament to good advice I don't know what is. At my age I am walking around like a Spring chicken without a care in the world. Almost every day I see men, of a similar age to me, limping around or tottering with broken knees on walkers or even in wheel chairs and I am thankful that I am not in as bad a shape as they are. I cannot imagine what it must be like not to be able to run or, for that matter, even walk naturally. As a person becomes older, ailments and injuries begin chipping away at the body and reduces the number of things that can be enjoyed. Like a very wise man once said to me, after he had both of his legs amputated and one eye removed, "Old age ain't for sissies."

Incidentally, I have recently heard that Sarasota has a newly formed rugby club called the Saracens. After the demise of the two previous ventures, the Red Tide and the Exiles , I wish them every success in their venture and hope that they will flourish. Perhaps I should connect them with my Welsh friends who run the Newport Saracens in the hope that these teams can perhaps arrange some matches between each other. The Welsh Saracens verses the Florida Saracens seems a natural to me and, let's face it, a Saracen victory is inevitable.

Twelve

The School of Hard Knocks

In my twenty five years of playing rugby, both in Wales and England, I took a lot of hard knocks and sustained some serious injuries. I completely shattered my lower jaw and I don't just mean unhinged it. I dislocated both of my shoulders which makes them susceptible to reoccur if they are hit in the correct place with any amount of force. I separately have broken my left collar bone and my right ankle which give me pain in cold climes. I have broken my nose three times which renders me with limited smelling power. I have had approximately a hundred stitches sewn into my head and face from various kicks and punches but none of this ever made me think that I should give up playing. I then came to America and began playing soccer which, for me, was literally a walk in the park. I received the usual bumps and bruises or the occasionally pulled or strained muscle but nothing that kept me from playing for more than a week or two. I had the advantage over soccer players because, if I collided with any of them, my rugby training kept me in good stead. The other unfortunate player, however, was usually laid out and I often would stay down on the floor pretending that I too was injured. Our trainer would run onto the pitch with his magic sponge but I would give him a sly wink just to let him know that I was only acting. The opposing player would then give me a wide berth, for the rest of the afternoon which allowed me all the time and space that I needed to do my work. However, when I took up the game again, at the age of sixty seven, although my attitude remained the same, my body did not have the same resilience that it once possessed. Consequently, I have taken quite a battering and my wife is crazy with thoughts of me seriously injuring myself. In spite of all this my hard man image still persists and the tales of my prowess are becoming legend amongst the younger players.

In one such incident a young player was coming towards the goal that I was defending and he inadvertently pushed the ball slightly farther from him than need be and I saw my opportunity. As he pulled back his leg to shoot at the goal I lunged in with my tackle. This situation, when both players hit the ball at the same time, is called a 50/50 ball and the force of me hitting the ball at the same time as he shot made him fly over the top of the ball. I came up with the ball and sailed on down the field on a counter attack. I never said anything at the time but with the force of him kicking the ball I felt a zigzag shock wave move up the shin bone of my left leg. I spoke to a professional athlete, some days later, and he told me that I was a fraction of force away from completely breaking my leg. His advice to me was that a man of my age should not be acting so recklessly and should probably think about retiring from all contact sports. On two other occasions I was drilled by an inexperienced player with the soccer ball, right in my private parts and this tends to slow you down somewhat. In each case I shouted to them that the ball was mine but neither of them had the sense to listen and drilled the ball with all their might. Talk about only fools and horses will not listen to common sense.

Another event happened when I was in front of the opponents goal and could see that one of my team mates was about to take a shot. As my experience taught me, I dropped to my knees to give him a better view of the goal. Needless to say he drilled me again with a fierce shot that hit me in the back of my head and almost decapitated me. This particular player was a professional and can hit the ball like shooting a cannon which left me dazed and it took several minutes for me to get my faculties back. Yet another time I did a flying header at a ball and after landing I almost dislocated my right elbow because the ground was so hard. Weeks later a long-time island resident told me that the old island air strip used to be located on the field where we now play and there was probably a layer of concrete hidden under the grass. This kind of information never seems to arise until after the fact.

Probably the worst incident was when I was playing on the same team as a Croatian player who weighed at least two hundred and fifty pounds. Earlier in the game he came up the field and passed me the ball. As he kept running I gave him a lovely through ball which he ran onto and shot on goal. I was standing on the left front side of the pitch, and not too far from where some of the players had parked their cars along the side line, when up the field he came again. In my mind I thought that the same play was on the cards and so I stood my ground awaiting for him to give me the ball so that I could play him in again. He kept coming and coming and never once looked up until before I knew it he barged head long into me and, with a huge crashing sound, he ran me into one of the parked cars. Then, to add insult to injury, after I hit the floor he then fell right on top of me. I am around a hundred pounds lighter than him and when his bulky frame came down on me it was like a boxer's one-two punch. I was knocked out for a short while and in the echoes of my mind I could hear someone shout for an ambulance to be called. As I began to come around and even before I stood up I shouted

"No ambulance". There was a few gasps from the younger players and a ripple of applause from the more experienced players because they didn't think that I would be able to stand up. Not only did I stand but to the amusement of all the players, a few minutes later, I joined back into the game as though nothing had happened. After that game one of the players came up to me and said that he didn't know if I was brave or completely crazy. Whichever the case he expressed that he would want me on any team that he played for because he knew that I would give everything that was in me to the team and the game.

Luckily, soccer is full of magical moments which, by far, outweigh the bad times. I sometimes reflect on some of the goals that I have scored throughout my career and as a younger man. I remember goals scored from my own half. I remember the flying headers, the back heals, the overhead bicycle kicks and the deft little flicks that all found their way into back of an opponents net. I once saw Ossie Ardilles, the Argentinean player, score a breath taking goal that was pure poetry. As he was running up the field, towards his opponents goal, the ball dropped behind him. Instead of bouncing over his head giving him the chance to volley it, the ball came down behind his back. Without breaking stride he flicked up his right heal and tap the ball over his own head and then as it looped over and dropped in front of him he shot it into the net. Now this is probably the best piece of improvisation that I think I have ever seen and it is even more impressive when it is considered that this was all done in a split second. This maneuver is virtually impossible to rehearse but it is something that must be in the back of a player's mind. When all the pieces of this play suddenly fall into place a player must realize that this option is on the cards. This very same play has happened to me twice in my lifetime and it was so exciting for everyone to see it unfold. It occurred once in outdoor soccer and once in indoor soccer and I executed them both stunningly. I did not score from either of these complicated volleys but, on both occasions, it brought a loud roar of appreciation from the spectators.

Just recently, in an in-house league, I was running up field when a ball bounced up and then was dropping down right in front of me. At that precise moment it was as if everything went into slow motion frames. I was just inside my own half of the field and I knew that the ball was going to be at exactly the height for a volley when I met it. I heard one of my teammates telling me to bring the ball down and control it but it was already too late. My brain told me to hit the ball and my shot took off at a high velocity of speed and whistled just over the cross bar, from some fifty yards away, with the goalkeeper hopelessly stranded. My teammate asked me why I took the shot and I replied that there is only a few times, in one's life, when a ball is naturally presented to a player for that kind of shot to be taken. I, for one, could not resist it and for having done so I will not apologize because it is brilliant moments like these that makes soccer so special. At my age it is a privilege to be able to, not only participate, but to remember what it feels like to be an achiever again. I am obviously a freak for my age but I have found that it is the mind that drives the body to perform when it should not be possible. I consider myself extremely fortunate that my forefathers gave me the genes that make it possible for me to do what others cannot. Some things can be achieved with smoke and mirrors but in the game of soccer there is no faking as everything is out in the open and you are what you are.

While in Wales recently I had Sunday lunch, with a group of friends at the famous Celtic Manor site of the most recent 2010 Ryder Cup golf match between Europe and the USA. On the next table to our group was the then Manager of Cardiff City Football Club. For the last two years this team has been knocked out of the Championship playoffs thus making their entrance to the revered Premiership Division impossible. This person was Dave Jones and upon finishing his meal he passed our table and I made a point of wishing him well even though I knew that his days with Cardiff were numbered. Well the inevitable happened and he was fired a short time later. I have often wondered why, when the players do not perform on the pitch, that it is inevitably the Manager who gets fired. I mean if a player fails to score a simple goal or fails to clear a ball out of defense and allows a goal because he is overawed by the occasion, how can it be the Manager's fault. High-salaried players must take ownership of their roles within the team and if they do not perform and produce the right results they should be dropped to the reserve team or fired. These playoff games should not be allowed anyway as the third-placed team should automatically go up and not have to play against the fourth, fifth and sixth position teams for that honor. If that was the case Cardiff would have been promoted the previous year as they finished in third position but after the playoffs, Blackpool, a team below them, went up instead. These additional games are only played to make extra money for the television company that has bought the rights to transmit them to millions of viewers. This is an extreme case of hysteria repeating itself.

Sharon and Lyn on their wedding day

Sharon "the Shark" Clarke

Lyn in trouble again

Sharon at her cutest

After Retirement

I always wanted to retire early and at sixty two that is exactly what I did. Although this meant that I would only get eighty percent of my Social Security I felt that I had enough money to see me through. Apart from which by taking the lesser amount I had worked out that it would be another thirteen years before my early retirement would work out against that decision and who knew if I would still be alive at that age. I bought my house when the market was low and that allowed me to pay for it with cash and not having a mortgage has saved me around sixty thousand dollars in interest payments. When working, I almost always had another job which gave me a second source of income and this was also my parachute incase the prime job went tits up. These second jobs always gave me a small amount of money until I found myself another primary income. I did exceptionally well in my last job which lasted six years and took me right up to the early retirement age that I had targeted. After retiring I only wanted to work part time as my savings paid for all my bills and this secondary income was my fun money. At first, here in Florida, I represented some Michigan companies owned by various friends of mine. This gave me an excuse, if I needed one, to visit many of Florida's nicer spots. Of course, I usually took my wife along and some of these deals were set up in her name which made her a minority business owner for tax purposes. This kept us going for about two years and then we stumbled upon the fact that the government had deregulated public pay phones and so we went out and bought six of them and installed them in low income trailer parks. In America, the people who use pay phones the most are Mexicans who want to talk to their families back home. Low class prostitutes also live in, or frequented these trailer parks which added to these colorful areas. I remember one day, in particular, when I was up on a ladder connecting some telephone wires. A hooker passed by and on seeing me she asked if there was anything she could do for me. With tongue in cheek I told her that she could hold the ladder to stop it from wobbling. Alas, my veiled attempt at humor was lost on this forlorn maiden and with a bemused look upon her face, she went about her business. After we came to know this business better we found out that we could have bought these items for half the cost if we had dealt directly with the telephone manufacturers. It took us five years to get our money back by which time collecting the money was becoming too dangerous to make it worthwhile. Slowly we pulled out of that business and sold all the phone parts to other small, local phone companies and the shrouds and pedestals to scrap metal businesses.

It was at this time that my wife and I got the writing bug. Sharon, since she was a teenager had always wanted to write a book and I had been told by various people that my life stories were worth writing about. So we now both plunged into this new venture. We brought out our first books, one each, around the middle of 2006 and between us we have now brought out one book per year, in the following five years, right up to this current book. It has been a great experience, for both of us, because it has taken our lives in a completely new direction and we have met a whole other group of people that we did not know even existed. Our book signings have taken us over to Britain and virtually to the four corners of the United States. In the past I have been strongly connected to sports and, to a lesser degree, the music industry but now I have exposed and immersed myself to a completely different culture. The sports and music scenes are populated with people of action but the writing business is full of thinkers and I, in turn, have benefited greatly from being a part of this culture. I have met other authors and shared their views. I have met cover designers and those who format books and learned to appreciate their work. I have met editors and have realized that my education, back in Britain, has made me capable of being able to do this myself and not have to pay for someone else to perform this function. I have also met printing and publishing companies and now have enough knowledge to know a good one from a bad one. To learn all of this has cost me money and the mistakes that I made in my early days have left me much wiser and more resilient. In fact my wife and I have now set up our own company to assist other new authors to self-publish their own books because if you are not a famous or exceptionally talented individual, no major publishing house will want to deal with you. There are literally thousands of regular people out there that want to publish their own stories and we offer them an inexpensive way of doing just that.

Because our books have a strong Welsh connection, our two main book selling trips are back to Wales and to the Welsh National Meeting which occurs once a year and is located in different cities around America each year. This coming year, over the Labor Day weekend it will be in Cleveland, Ohio. We will be packing up our car with books and other Welsh bric-a-brac which we take along to sell and ensure that our expenses are covered. I always make my trip back to Wales before the

Welsh Convention and this I do for a specific reason. In every town that I visit over there I go shopping and buy, as cheaply as possible, items of Welsh sentimental value. These items I then bring back to the USA and sell them, alongside our books, making our trips to these functions more plausible. I have customers who request that I look for specific items that they cannot find themselves. Most of these people can never, for numerous reasons, make a trip back to the Mother Land and so they have to live vicariously through travellers like myself. I buy flags, miner's lamps, military badges, toasting forks, brass figures, souvenir plates and other china bits and pieces and carry them all back to America in my suitcase. I use the same suitcase in which I carried my books to Wales at the beginning of my trip. I schlep books to Wales and souvenirs back to America. I have been asked on many occasions why is it that I carry the books with me on the flight over and there is a simple answer to that mysterious question. I just cannot find any printing company, in Britain, that can get anywhere near the price that I pay for my books here in America. I am talking as much as three times more and this makes buying my books in Britain out of the question. So, as long as I am physically able, our books are going to be put on a plane and due to the fact that on overseas flights you are allowed one suitcase free, it really doesn't cost me a dime. I hope that the money saved will not be offset, somewhere in the future, by the cost of a hernia operation. In my life style this would be considered an occupational hazard and, to further emphasize this point, my motto has always been that a person should work to live and not live to work.

When I travel to Britain I am always asked by my soccer playing buddies to bring back various team shirts and memorabilia . This is also a source of revenue because I search for items which are on sale and sell them at the list price. No one ever queries the price because they could never make the trip themselves and they are so pleased to own an item from their favorite soccer club. Of course, all the big clubs like Manchester United, Liverpool, Arsenal, Chelsea, etc. are in high demand but sometimes a person will ask me to bring back some of the less famous club's shirt as they would prefer to wear something that no one else owns. Another thing that I look for is old, out of print books. For these I go to the local town markets as these items usually turn up there. I am not always certain what I am looking for until I see it and sometimes it can be an impulse buy brought on by a faint long lost memory. I was on one of these reconnoitre operations with my wife at my side when she picked up an old bible and when she opened it a written name inside caught her eye. The name was Homer and it was significant to her because that was her father's name. The dog-eared bible was about a hundred and fifty years old and was obviously a book that had been in the possession of one particular family for many generations. There was another particular name, handwritten in pen inside the cover, which was George Sankey and it was dated 1868. There were other names such as Sarah Hodnett and an address which was 31, Lonsdale Road, off Crown Street, Liverpool. The market, where we found this bible was at my home town of Pontypool almost two hundred miles south of Liverpool and it seemed strange that this bible would end up so far away from home. We returned to Florida and when we next went to visit my wife's dad in Michigan we presented him with the tattered and torn bible. Unfortunately, Sharon's dad passed away about two years later and after the funeral Sharon retrieved the old relic and brought it back to Florida. Some months later she received a phone call from one of her nephews and he asked if he could buy the bible from her but Sharon turned down his offer. This particular nephew is very seriously religious and had recognized the name of George Sankey as being the cohort of another famous early Evangelist here in America, a man named D.L. Moody. Apparently the afore named Mr. Sankey had moved his family to America and linked up with Moody then travelled the U.S.A. preaching their evangelistic brand of religion across the whole continent. For a spell of about thirty years they were famous throughout this country as being the leading lights for spreading their Evangelistic faith. People would travel from miles around to hear their fire and brimstone brand of sermons. I have the thought that one of these days I should Google the name of George Sankey and see if I can trace any remnants of his family. Even better, I should contact the television program *The History Detectives* because this type of thing is right up their alley.

Where I now live is full of surprises and when I dig in my yard it is quite likely that I will find a shark tooth or two. All these barrier islands have about two foot of earth on top of sand and so you don't have to dig very deep before you will be uncovering various sea shells and the occasional shark's tooth. On rarer occasions even a megladon tooth can be found and with this prehistoric shark growing to about forty foot long you can imagine how big the teeth are. Around my neck I wear a fossilized great white shark's tooth which is at least a couple of thousand years old. This my wife and I found on the beach near our house when we were walking the shore line in about a foot of water. About five years ago, in their infinite wisdom, our local commissioners decided that our beaches needed re-nourishing and to that end they hired a company to dredge off shore sand and pump it up onto the beaches. Since then it has become a lot more difficult to find sharks teeth of any notable size. In a few more years what with the waves and tides gently sifting the sand, it will become easier to find these nuggets of historical significance. Some people have been lucky enough to have found an odd piece of Spanish gold because the Gulf of Mexico has taken many a galleon into its bosom. These incidents are few and far between but just imagine the excitement of finding a coin which is around five hundred years old and is valuable almost beyond belief. These are the types of things that, living in a paradise like this, are not only pleasurable but they come with an inevitable air of unbridled anticipation from one day to the next. In the stages of my life I have not always made the right decisions but I thank my lucky stars that, in the matter of moving to live here, my decisions has balanced out and made up for all those other misguided choices.

Fourteen

Weird and Wonderful

Just over on the mainland in Bradenton, no more than ten miles away from where I live, they now have a women's roller skating derby team. They are aptly named the Bradentucky Bombers and it was my experience to witness one of their matches about two years ago. It was mid February and my soccer playing buddies from Michigan were in town for their winter break and they were at a loose end for something to do. I had seen an advertisement in the local newspaper and just mentioned it as a possible diversion from the usual types of entertainment that we participated in. At first my suggestion was laughed at but as the afternoon beers took affect this option began to seem more appealing and even a realistic possibility. We decided to go and this would be something a little on the dark side but would amuse our weird senses of humor.

Well, the dark side turned out to be nothing short of Gothic. I have never seen so many tattoos and body piercing on women in my life. These were not demure ladies, these were bitches from hell and this is a title that they entirely embraced. Now I have seen this type of sport briefly on the television and even in some old movies but to physically be there is another whole different kettle of fish. These tough broads fly around a track, on skates, trying to demolish the opposing team by any means that they can, no holds barred. There were elbows flying, shoulders crashing and feet tripping at anyone from the visiting Fort Myers team that these marauding skaters came across. The crowd really got into the match as well what with yelling, cheering and booing incessantly at what sometimes seemed for no other reason but to heighten the blood feud on the track. The supporters were an unusual bunch of people sporting multi-colored Mohawk hairstyles and a myriad of industrial chains dripping from their leather jackets. Some even had their faces pierced with all kind of ornamental objects hanging from them. Well the Michigan guys wanted to experience something different and this event was just about as different as it could be. The old saying "The people you meet when you haven't got your gun, " came to mind, but as we all are too well aware, you can't shoot them, there's a law against it. More power to this gallant venture because throughout the night, even with all the carnage and mayhem ensuing all around, I did not see the slightest bit of trouble and if that is not a plus, I don't know what is. I wish them well and long may their carbuncles fester.

Here's a weird one for you. In the mighty fine state of Oklahoma the people there have invented what must be one of the strangest pastimes ever. The people from that state refer to themselves as Okies, as in the song *I'm an Okie from the Muskogee*, and they have contrived to come up with a new sport which they have named Okie Noodling. In the dictionary the word "noodle" is described as a flour based food mainly used in soup " or the other definition is "a Simpleton. " However, I am told that the more likely explanation is that it is a derivative of the term "canoodling" which is a jargon in some parts for getting close to somebody, or in this particular case, something. The folk down there get into the rivers dressed in nothing more than a pair of blue-jeans and a wife beater shirt, the style with the sleeves cut off, and proceed to catch catfish with their bare hands. They search the river banks mainly with their head above water but their hands under the water and feel around for catfish holes. The catfish that they are looking for are the big ones that snap back when disturbed. By annoying these catfish the "noodlers" are hoping that, in snapping, the catfish will lock onto their hand and then they can lift the fish out of the water. The catfish they are trying to catch can be up to four feet long and weigh around seventy to eighty pounds and will keep the average Okie family fed for a week. This seems to me to have come about as a poor man's need because there is absolutely no equipment used in this process. Somewhere a man out there in the boonies was so desperate for food that he knew where a catfish was and just jumped in and wrestled that son-of-a-gun right out of there. He probably told a few of his buddy's and they also tried it. Now it has developed into a sporting contest and these people come from near and far to see who can catch the biggest catfish. Of course, after the competition, they fry those babies up and all the families, who have come for the day out, gets a heeping helping of southern hospitality. Don't be at all surprised to see Okie Noodling at the Olympic Games in years to come as America likes nothing better than to introduce a sport that only they are good at. You might thing my views on this subject are slightly jaundiced but you only have to look at skateboarding and synchronized swimming to get my drift. After all, didn't America invent the bigger tennis racquet, the bigger golf ball and the long handled putter for that very purpose. I can see those good ole boys standing up there on the podium receiving their medals, all dressed up like Tool Man Tim clad in their jeans, baseball caps and wife beater shirts. I can even picture the Olympic Organization allowing The Battle Hymn of the Republic to be played, at the ceremony instead of the Star Spangled Banner. *YeeHaw*, as predicted, the south will rise again.

I saw a funny sign in the men's toilet of the local island Moose Lodge which I frequent. It was mounted directly over the urinals and said in big bold letters "Please stand closer to avoid peeing on the floor." Correct me if I am wrong but doesn't this affliction occur around about the same time as a man's eyes begin to fail him? Most of these gentlemen would have to step back to read the sign and consequently end up peeing on the floor more often than before the sign was put there. The counter-productivity of this sign and its consequences must have dawned on the signee because it has disappeared from view. In the same men's toilet in the same Moose Club I went in to, ahem, powder my nose. Not thinking I set my drink down in the wash basin which triggered the automatic hand faucet which immediately dumped a load of water into my glass of beer. I forgot that the faucets were activated by censors which turn on, primarily when you go to wash your hands. I don't mind the hand towels being operated by sensors but not the faucets. I mean that could have been an expensive glass of Brandy or a malted Scottish whisky. Incidently, have you ever noticed that Irish brands of this elixir are spelled "whiskey." Yet another snippet of useless information that you can roll out when there is one of those a pregnant pauses at the next cocktail party that you attend. It is guaranteed to suck the oxygen right out of the room. Oh, when smoking was allowed at the Moose the participants would all sit at one end of the bar coughing their lungs up. I amusingly named that area Coffin Corner. Remember, just because a person is uneducated doesn't automatically make him stupid.

Another stranger than fiction sight is at Captain Tony's

Bar down in Key West, Florida where the Gulf of Mexico meets the Atlantic Ocean. Cemented into the floor is a grave yard headstone which is something that is rarely seen in the course of one's life. Apparently Captain Tony was a bit of a rascal and for many years he had an affair with a married lady from that town. Eventually, and after her death, the husband found out about this tryst and was so enraged that he went to the cemetery and dug up the head stone. The man then drove to Captain Tony's Bar and flung the head-stone through the door, which I am told was closed at the time. He then yelled to the captain that he had been with her in life and now he could be with her in death. It would be wrong of me to mention the lady's name but it is plain for anyone to read if you choose to visit this quaint but notorious place. Tony's place is one of a kind what with all the lady's brassieres hanging from the rafters. If you buy one of their embossed plastic cups it will cost a little more but whenever you return any time in the future that cup, when presented, will afford you discounted drinks forever and a day. Tony grew up and caroused with an icon of mine, the well known writer Earnest Hemmingway, another reprobate of the same order. Things must have gotten pretty wild when those two delinquents began to party in that most southern location of the continental United States.

While on the subject of amusingly wild events, I once had to organize a party for a group of my best customers. My boss, the Sales Director, was due to attend but he left all the detailed arrangement to me. I always got a kick out of seeing people's surprised looks when, as I often did, I would pull one of my outrageous pranks. For this particular party I hired a stripper but I asked her to come dressed as a typical business woman and I would introduce her to my boss as one of the customers. At the shank of the evening and when every-one was suitably well oiled I gave the stripper the signal for her to begin her deception. She seductively started to dance and, at the same time, slowly and deliberately began to take her garments off one at a time. Now, my boss, thinking that she was a respectable customer gone bad, began to squirm and fidget. He kept glancing at me with a frightened look as if to plead that I should put a stop to this charade. After what seemed an inaudible length of time she was down to her bra and panties and at this point my boss rushed over and threw his jacket around her and bustled her out of the room. About five minutes later he came back into the room beaming from ear to ear. The stripper had informed him of our little ruse and he felt a good deal happier knowing that she was, after all, not one of our customers. Everyone in attendance had a good laugh at this extraordinary set of circumstances and my boss never did come to another of these functions. I don't know whether he was afraid of being sued or whether another trick, like this one, could literally give him a heart attack. As we say, here in America, "If you can't run with the big dogs then stay on the porch." This reminds me that I once met a stripper from Padukah, Kentucky whose name was, wait for it...Ralph.

A good, old buddy of mine was frequently known to over-imbibe and when these occasions arose he would end up in all sorts of strange circumstances. On one particular night, at a rather posh hotel, he found himself, yet again, in that unenviable of all situations. It had been a long hard day of drinking and as the twilight hours were approaching he decided to take a nap. The only place where he thought that he could take refuge was under the table at which he and his inebriated gang of rugby players were sitting. He was soon deep in the arms of slumber and the next thing that he knew was that someone was rudely kicking him. When he finally got his head together he then realized that he was still under the table after what seemed like a prolonged period of time. He thought that he would surprise his pals but when he arose, from his hibernation, there was a whole different group of people around the table. The table was now fully furnished with food, cutlery and china while this new set of people were tucking into a substantial meal. Then the penny dropped, he realized that he had slept right through the night and the new set of diners were in fact the hotel's guests who were partaking of a hearty breakfast. He received some real old fashioned looks as he crawled through their legs and stumbled to his feet. He didn't complain or explain because no words could describe the details that led him to this embarrassing situation. He just wryly smiled and headed out for the door. All his drunken friends had gone home with not a thought of waking him up and here he was thirty miles from home and having stayed out all night. This took a good deal of explaining to his wife when he finally arrived home, some twenty four hours after he had left, on the previous evening. Of course, all his cohorts had a good laugh for weeks to come at his expense as instances such as these were merely written off as acceptable by the hardened rugby drinking fraternity.

Fifteen

Inevitably, Life Goes On

In the past two years, on this island, we have had a large amount of unusual things to contend with. Miss Jackie, who owns the Paradise Café, was told that she had to move her business because the landlord was knocking down the building plus three others around her. This was being done to accommodate Walgreens, a chain of drug stores, who are to build a large stand-alone store at the end of the block where she was situated. It only meant us moving about four doors down the block and, at least, this was to take place during June which is an off season month. Never-the-less this was a stressful and worrying time for her. We closed at the old café location at 2:00 PM on a Thursday afternoon and began the move. We all worked furiously, nonstop that evening and I must have made a hundred trips back and forth, moving dolly loads of items until late into that night. The next day, which was Friday, we worked all day from sunup to sundown and virtually moved every thing but the kitchen sink. We did not need that item because we had a brand new one already in place. On Saturday morning bang on 7:00 AM we were serving breakfast at our new location and everyone was absolutely amazed at what we had achieved. As it happens, Miss Jackie, is now located in a better spot and business appears to have picked up quite considerably. Her place now has a newer, fresher look than the old place and even has a café area and a separate dining area. The new location has allowed us to be better organized and more professional. The service that she now provides is more streamlined and convenient for the customers. A good job was done by all and it appears to be a win/win situation.

I could not very well talk about this region without mentioning the simply horrific explosion on the British Petroleum's *Deep Water Horizon* oil rig off the Gulf of Mexico's Louisiana coastline. Where I live is around three hundred miles, as the crow flies, to the southeast of this disastrous event and it did not adversely affect this area. Because of the prevailing tides and winds the oil slick which this catastrophe unleashed came ashore all along the Louisiana, Mississippi, Alabama and western part of the Florida Panhandle shores. BP has worked long and hard to rectify this bad situation and in many cases they have made restitution and compensated for the damage which they have caused. However, some peoples lives and businesses will never be the same. Mother Nature has a way of healing herself but it will, in some areas, take many insufferable years. Some of the rich oyster beds will be contaminated for years to come and some small family owned companies may never recover. The older business owners will not have the time, or in some cases the heart, to start all over again and some have already called it a day. It is like getting kicked in the stomach, when you are already on your knees, it is just too hard to recover. Some of these little companies have been operating for generations and never gave a thought to the fact that one day, BAM!, right out of the blue, their business would be taken away with no fault of their own. I have seen this happen before, back in Wales, to the coal and steel industry but that was over a period of several years. In this case some people were in business one day and out of business the next. My heart goes out to those people and it is because now their many happy times are just mere memories.

People were also killed on that oil rig when it blew up. I think about these workers from time to time and one young man in particular jogs my memory. I met him in a local American Legion Club where he was attending a wedding. My wife and I were in an adjacent bar room in the same building when he came sauntering in. He wanted to get away from the country music that they were incessantly playing as it was just about driving him insane. We got to talking with him and he bought us a couple of drinks and in return I gave him a copy of my first book. He had told me that he was an underwater maintenance welder on the rigs and worked two weeks on and two weeks off. During his two weeks on he had to stay under water, in some sort of a bathysphere and for those occasions he was always looking for books to read. I asked him to promise me that he would take my book underwater with him and he said that he would do so. I only hope that this brave young man was not involved in that horrendous incident. I didn't ask his name and so I have no way to check on this. I don't often meet young men who are honest and forthright, but this young man was and not only that, he was true to himself. Not all of today's young people have character but this man was one that, once met, would never be forgotten.

Nowhere in the world is completely safe as we found out, to our chagrin, about six months ago. Two young male British tourists came over and were staying on the next island down from us called Longboat Key. They decided to go for a night out in Sarasota which is a city around twenty miles from here with a wonderful, carefree reputation. It is a ritzy kind of place backed by a lot of new money and has its own opera house, ballet company and generally it is a glamorous, artsy kind of city. These two promising young men had a good night out, by all accounts, but somehow they ended up in the worst part of this town and were both shot dead. This particular part of town is teeming with prostitutes and drug traffickers and does not seem to fit into these young men's background. Nevertheless, there they were and no one seems to know how or why they ended up in this particular area but the outcome was tragic and fatal. There has been a good deal of speculation as to how they met their demise but, I guess, we will never really know how this episode went down. Since they were observed by security cameras to be in quite a few different bars that night, perhaps alcohol impaired their judgment. Alternatively, maybe someone slipped a drug into their drinks unbeknownst to them and so the conjecture is endless. They could have been lured there or just got lost but, whichever was the case, the result ended up the same. The sixteen year old African American teenager who murdered them was out of jail under his mother's supervision, after a previous shooting incident and he should never have been on the streets that night. Perhaps he tried to rob them and they, not having ever been in such a sordid occurrence, unwisely fought back. Here in America, because of the gun situation, people generally know not to resist a robbery and the advice given by the law enforcement community is to just hand over your wallet. If these two men fought back this might have frightened the perpetrator and caused him to shoot them. This whole incident has left all of us in these parts with a black eye and has enforced the belief that we still have to warn visitors to take taxis to and from their destinations. No matter how affluent a place appears to be on the surface we must always be aware the there is inevitably a criminal minority lurking around in the shadows. Which ever Judge allowed the assail-ant to stay on the streets to be a further menace to society must be ruing his decision and probably does not sleep too well at night. This whole episode could prevent some tourists from coming to this region of Florida, which is a pity because it really is an amazing place to visit. The families of these two young men must be devastated and the only glimmer of hope to come out of the whole affair is that perhaps someone else will learn from this tragedy to always air on the cautious side.

Unfortunately, death is no stranger to our paradise island either and just last week we had two such fatalities. One was where a woman, in her mid-fifties was found floating out in the Gulf on a large boogie board. When the Coast Guard reached her she was already dead and although the results of an autopsy have not yet surfaced, it looks very much as if she had a heart attack. The second was of a three hundred pound man who plummeted into the sea from a height of eight hundred feet. He was parasailing when the boat that was towing him stalled and, consequently, the parachute folded causing him to drop. The impact of him hitting the water from that height was like him hitting concrete and I am pretty sure this caused his fate. About five years ago two men were flying an ultra-lite plane when a strut, supporting one of the wings, snapped causing the wing to collide with the rear-mounted engine which caused them to drop like a rock, right into the shallow waters. They actually came down near the beach adjacent to my house and I witnessed their bodies, under tarps, on the sand. It was the passenger's birthday and his girlfriend paid for the one hour ride as a gift to him. Not only that, she was on the beach and witnessed the whole incident. Riptides after storms, here on the islands, are another source of danger and one which most visitors have never experienced. These can quite often prove to be deadly because they suck unsuspecting swimmers out to sea where they drown. We have had accidental diving deaths when people think that the water is deeper than it actually is. We have had driving deaths, one when a car happened to hit the drawbridge after it began to go up and another when a guy drove right over the bridge's side railing and dropped thirty feet into the Inter Coastal Waterway. We have had people falling over board from speedboats to sailing vessels and have drowned because they were, for some foolish reason, not wearing a life jacket. We have had at least half a dozen cases where a couple have broken up and, usually the man, decides that he is going to commit a murder/suicide pact and takes them both out. We have had both tourists and local people die from accidental drug overdoses and we have had people commit their own deliberate suicide. All these details make the islands appear to be a dangerous place to live but so long as you have your wits about you and do not throw caution to the wind, this is still one of the best places in the world to live.

As I am writing, it is June and the jellyfish are migrating. I am not completely certain if they are heading north or south along the coastline but I have heard that already a couple of a hundred jellyfish stings have been reported. There are many types of jellyfish, with the most notorious being the Portuguese Man of War, however, they all sting to some extent or other and should be avoided at all costs. Even when they are washed up on the beach and appear dead they can still sting you. If you feel inclined to touch them make sure that you do so with a stick and never pick one up. In the water they are the most dangerous because they are so transparent that they are very nearly invisible. In the ocean, their tentacles can stretch up to six feet long and it is with these that they stun fish and thus catch their food. My wife Sharon, when she was eight years old, swam into a swarm of jelly fish, over on the Atlantic Coast and was stung all over. She was sick and laid up in bed for three days and this is not something that anyone wants especially when on vacation. This is just another message from Mother Nature to remind us that she is still very much in charge and that her vengeance will be exacted upon anyone that does not heed her warnings. I am told that an old cure for such stings is to pour urine on the affected areas. I, for one, think that I would prefer to apply a more conventional medication because I would rather be pissed off than pissed on. I have so many jokes it is not even funny.

About six years ago Anna Maria Island lost a local man who most people know but had never actually seen as a hero. I am referring to Ralph Russell the now deceased owner of Rotten Ralph's bar and restaurant. Ralph was an unsung hero because of an act of bravery when he and his wife Doreen were on vacation in Ireland and this little known fact only received a small amount of publicity in the local press. The Russell family loved to go over to the old country and go off the beaten track looking for old castles and rare sights. On one such trip they were on a two-lane country road following another car as it was impossible to over take. Suddenly, and for some inexplicable reason the car in front strayed into the oncoming lane right at the crest of a hill. The timing could not have been worse because it was hit head on by a large truck. It was a horrific crash but Ralph stopped his car about thirty yards from this tragedy and ran over to render any help that he could. Alas, the father, mother and their teenaged son and daughter were all killed on impact. As Ralph stood next to the car, trying to take in everything that had just happened, he notice some movement from under a pile of clothes on the backseat. Realizing that there was someone still alive in the car he frantically wrestled to open the doors but to no avail. He then saw that the hatch at the back of the car was unlocked and gained entry. He lifted the pile of clothes and there he found a small, three year old boy. He dragged the child out to safety and within a few minutes the car exploded into flames and was burned to a cinder. A nurse appeared on the scene and took care of the young boy until the police and ambulance arrived and whisked him away. The Irish police later contacted Ralph to let him know that the boy was on the mend and to assure him that the other four poor souls had been killed on impact and did not suffer in the inferno which enveloped that car. The next day he went to see the wrecked car and there was virtually nothing left of it. A few days after the tragedy, one of the leading Irish newspapers ran a front page story about the American tourist who went out of his way to save a young boy's life. About a week later Ralph was back at his restaurant, on Bimini Bay, and was meeting and greeting customers as if nothing out of the ordinary had happened. I sat and had a drink with him one night and it was then that he told me this story. He was a big but gentle man with a kind heart and a broad smile. It is not too often that a person gets to meet a real hero face to face and it is now obvious that Rotten Ralph, as his moniker belies, was not rotten after all.

The holy gates to Liverpool's Anfield Ground

Sharon, daughter Danielle and granddaughter Brooke
with Mickey Mouse

Lyn at War Memorial gates in Pontypool

Lyn with the Ryder Cup

Sixteen

Still Traveling

I have just returned from what must be my thirty fifth visit to Wales and England in the past thirty five years. One year I did not go at all, however, on another year I flew over there twice. Unless you have lived in different countries you have nothing to compare how things are in other places but take it from me, just about everything is smaller over there. Cars are generally smaller, as are houses and so are, consequently rooms, baths, showers, kitchens and so on. Stores are in most part smaller and so are shops, post offices, bars, cafes, restaurants and even the doctors office. Every thing tends to close earlier in the evening and on some days they don't open at all or for only half a day and in various towns those days are different. They drive on the other side of the road and because of that the steering wheel is on the other side of the car. I am always trying to get into the wrong side of the car over there and when I find myself doing this I kick the tire on that side to pretend that I am over there for some legitimate reason. The water faucets turn the opposite way and the electric light switches go down for off instead of up. In very old houses the doors are so narrow to such an extent that a person has a heck of a job trying to get a modern standard piece of furniture into a house. Nevertheless, the people of Britain carry on with a stiff upper lip and all these inconveniences are taken in stride. A good number of them walk around coughing or sniffling but no one will ever admit that they have a cold. Apparently it is just some minor problem that they have been dealing with for most of their lives. No matter how hard that I try not to, I always catch a cold on my visits over there and I could not, by any means, be considered a sickly person. The weather over there mostly changes three times in one day and because it is farther north it has daylight at around 6:00 AM and is still light at 11:00 PM in the summer. After living in America since 1976, all what was normal to me before then, now seems peculiar. Please understand that this is not a carping session, it is just to explain how different the two cultures are and how my views on this subject have changed. The one thing that has not changed, however, is the kind hearted people that you meet on a daily basis in every walk of life. Thousands of years have gone into the building of their character and American visitors must remember that because we have only been a nation for what they consider the blink of an eye, we are still very much the new kids on the block. Although some things are annoying I still get a thrill when visiting this tiny land and if my health remains good I will probably be back there again next year.

Each individual time that I revisit the United Kingdom there are always some incidents or places that linger in my mind and in some cases they bring a broad smile to my face. My children, Louise and Richard, and I accompanied my good friend Joe Byrne on one of his karaoke nights over in Liverpool. Joe picked me up by car, from the Bridge Inn Hotel in Port Sunlight, while the kids came over by train from West Kirby. We met up at The Grapes, a well known pub on Matthew Street in the heart of downtown Liverpool. The Grapes is less than a hundred yards away from another place made famous by The Beatles, I am talking about The Cavern Club. We arrived there about 7:00 PM and even this early, it was standing room only. Luckily a hen party of girls, hellbent on drinking Liverpool dry, moved on to their next watering hole and we were all able to sit right next to the stage. The singers varied from good to bad but the good ones were exceptionally good. One guy sang only Englebert Humperdink songs while a woman from Southport did excellent renditions of Patsy Cline classics. Joe, my old rugby team buddy, did his usual collection of Frank Sinatra oldies and had the whole crowd singing along with him. It is amazing that in Britain so many pubs have gone out of business. For instance in Caerleon, where I stay in Wales, two bars have shut their doors since my last visit and in Pontypool, my home town, there are only a handful of pubs left where once there was one on every corner. Their demise has been brought about by the strict drinking and driving laws, the smoking bans and the price of cheap beer which can now be bought at any liquor store. In spite of all this, there are pockets around the country that still remain strong and Matthew Street, and in particular places like The Grapes, is the exception to the rule. We had a fabulous night and after my kids caught the last train back to West Kirby, Joe and I finished off the night with a quiet drink at a different watering hole with that good singer that I mentioned earlier, Jonny G. My twisted, Mr. Joe had told Jonny that I was a talent scout from America and I was looking for acts to take back to Florida and Jonny wasn't going to let me out of his sight. Forty odd years ago Joe and I were always pulling scams such as this and I must admit that it did garner us a goodly sum of free drinks. Joe has slowed down somewhat but he still has a gleam in his eye and an unbroken spirit and this is what keeps people like Joe and me on top of our game.

Down in Wales there is an amazing man who I have become friendly with over the past years. His name is Doctor Russell Rees and not only is he a doctor but he is a successful business man, a property owner and an antique dealer. He has been a local politician, a debater, an historian, an inquisitor and a great influence to many people. He occasionally likes to share an early evening bottle of wine with me and picks my brain for information as to what is happening across the pond. He is in his mid-eighties and he is as inquisitive now as he was when I first made his acquaintance almost thirty years ago. When I first met him he was in Atlanta, Georgia a with the Newport Saracens Rugby Club who were there on tour. He came down from his room one night, looking dapper from his napper to his feet, when one of those rambunctious Saracens threw him right into the swimming pool, fully clothed. He took that incident in good fun but he stayed away from swimming pools for the rest of that tour. In his hometown of Caerleon he is fondly referred to as Doctor Woodworm by the locals. This came about because when he made house calls, as is the custom over there if a patient is too ill to get to the doctor's office, he always had his eyes open for any tasty bits of antique furniture. All this is said with a tongue-in-cheek attitude as in Wales they only make these kind of open jokes about people that they admire and respect. The Doc has always liked me and has often said that I remind him of himself when he was a younger man. He will frequently introduce me to others and follows this up by telling them, with a modicum of pride, that I am over from America promoting my own books. He has, from time to time, also told me that if I lived permanently in Wales that he could see the two of us getting involved in some project or another as partners. This, to me, is no small compliment and it is reassuring to think that a man who has had so much success in his life, would speak of me in such glowing terms.

Just before the Ryder Cup came to that area I told him that all the small restaurants and cafes should come together under one huge tent on the town's central green. This would make it so much easier for foreign golf fans to find them and taste their wares at leisure. He thought that this was a great idea and asked me to return there prior to the event and help him organize this. Unfortunately, this venture did not get off the ground because the Borough of Newport annexed Caerleon and promptly set about making sure that the business owners of that town were completely left out of this once in a lifetime opportunity. They cut off the town from this prestigious event by closing the road from the town to the Celtic Manor thus ensuring that the avid golf followers did not get the chance to see this historic place. I really admire this lovable old rogue and I hope that I will meet him again in the not too distant future, When he finally leaves this planet, as we all must one day, he will be sorely missed and never replicated. His parting will leave this world a sadder place but the memory of him will kindle warmly and perpetuate for many years to come. When a genie is let out of his bottle it is impossible to ever get it back in.

On my last weekend of my recent visit to Wales, I was invited to stay with our good friends Lyndsey and Annette Lewis. Knowing that I love to delve into historic places they took me for a little drive over to a place near where they live called Llantwit Major but more specifically to the church of Saint Illtuds. This is a revered site for the Celtic people who were prominent in Wales thousands of years ago and long before the Romans came to that land just after the birth of Christ. The actual name for this historic place is Llanilltud Fawr meaning the great church of Illtud. This church has stood on this site since around the year 500 AD which is just at the end of the reign of the magnificent Welsh king Arthur whose legends have stirred the imagination ever since. When the Angles and Saxons invaded what is now England, Christianity was kept alive by saints such as Illtud who travelled by sea between Wales, Brittany, Cornwall and Ireland spreading the gospel. He came from the valley of the Ogney Brook and built his church there, which also contained a monastery, school and a mission center. From here, the early priests went out and built more churches throughout the Celtic kingdom and so Llantwit Major was the hub of the Christian world of that period. The original church fell into ruin but the Normans, who came to these parts around 1066 AD, rebuilt it out of stone and it has lasted to this day.

The church, as it can be seen today, is actually two churches joined together. The West church is the Norman half and the East church was added about two hundred years later. I think that the most interesting thing about this site is that contained in the West church are Celtic rune stones, as tall as six feet and totally inscribed with Celtic designs and words. These stones are around fifteen hundred years old and should not be missed. The old Curfew Bell from the town is also located here and it is inscribed with the words: *Saint Illtud pray for us.* Outside, at the back of the church, are the burial places of local kings and are signified by Celtic crosses. Saint Illtud and another abbot of that period, named Sampson, are also buried here. People most assuredly drive past this sight on a daily basis and are blissfully unaware of the great, early significance of locations rich in history such as this one. This is typical of the sorts of places that I love to go to when I visit my homeland. Lyndsey and I had a great time the previous day in Cardiff, when we went to see the rugby match between Wales and the Barbarians who are basically the pick of the world team. Yet it is the trip to the church of Saint Illtud that will stand out, in my mind, for many years to come. Remember now, King Arthur *was* a real king who stopped the Hun invaders from swarming in and taking over all of Britain after the retreat of the Romans. He fought many battles against them and, having won, succeeded in restricting these vandals to the outer edges of the country which they called Angland.

Seventeen

Blasts from the Past

My wife and I are members of the Sarasota Welsh Society and for the past five years we have attended their annual Saint David's Day dinners which occurs on the first of March. Though always enjoyable affairs, this year's event was by far the best. Due, in part, to the urging our friend, Colin Mayled, the organizing committee was persuaded to shell out some funds for good entertainment, which was a landmark first. Now, this proved very opportunistic because Colin had a long time acquaintance from his Welsh home town of Abergavenny who could fit this bill and just so happened to be staying in Orlando about a two hour car ride from Sarasota. He was none other than the well known Welsh born entertainer, Bryn Yemm, and he was a perfect candidate for this job. Colin and Bryn grew up and ran the streets together as boys and even though their lives had taken different paths over the years they always stayed in touch. Well, Bryn was hired and Colin, myself and our wives shared a table with Bryn and his wife and we all enjoyed the fine meal and the amusing banter which accompanied it. After dinner Bryn put on a floor show of songs interspersed with funny stories that back home in Wales one would have to line up for tickets and pay good money to see. The whole crowd of around two hundred people were entertained by a man who had been a top line act in the old country for thirty odd years. When I have spoken of this to other Welsh people, some have told me that each Christmas, after dinner, they would all sit around and play Bryn's music. At the end of the night Bryn gave Sharon and I one of his latest CDs and we in turn gave him one each of our books. A fair swap I would say as all parties were satisfied.

During the course of dinner that night Bryn told us an amazing story. He was born to a teenaged, unwed girl from the town of Brynmawr and shortly after his birth she was crying while walking around with baby Bryn in her arms. She ended up at a bus stop and had absolutely no idea what she was going to do or where she was going to stay. While at the bus stop she met a kind woman who tried to comfort her but she was beyond her wits end with worry. Finally, the kind lady said that if the young girl would give the baby to her she would ensure that it would have a good home and be loved and cared for. The teenager relented because she felt that this would be better than anything that she could offer to her newborn child. The woman, as it turned out, was a member of the Salvation Army and she took the infant Bryn to her sister in Abergavenny where he was lovingly brought up in a charitable household. People often talk about fate and how "What is meant to be will be," but on some occasions the true facts are still stranger than fiction. Bryn was raised within that charitable faith and even now many of the songs that he performs are hymns. He tells this story, about that stroke of divine intervention into his life, to anyone who is willing to listen because he feels that it is significant to how his life was changed and what he has since become. The one song above all that I will remember him singing that evening, was *How Great Thou Art* because he sung it with such conviction. Although I am not a deeply religious person, for some unknown reason, probably the way he sung it, the song resounded deeply within me. Well, I must say that he is a joy to be around and I hope that we will meet again one day because his kind of sincerity is a breath of fresh air in these times of uncertainty and mistrust.

Around three years ago Sharon and I flew over to Wales for the wedding of our friends daughter, Rachel. It was a wonderful occasion and, as could be expected, no expense was spared by the Lewis' of Talygarn. We were again invited, this past Christmas, to the wedding of their second and youngest daughter, Sarah. Unfortunately, due to our family commitments we were unable to attend which was a real shame because it was a blast. Earlier this year, Lyndsey and Annette came back over to their house at Cortez, here in Florida. As usual my wife and I were invited over one evening for a dinner party. As the night wound down Annette asked if we would like to see the video of Sarah's wedding to which we avidly agreed. We were all sitting there watching the film when the camera panned around and over to the singer/pianist who was supplying the entertainment. I immediately recognized him as being a young man who Sharon and I had met several years earlier when he was playing at the Celtic Manor. His name is Richard Harris [not the actor who used to carouse with Richard Burton and Peter O'Toole] and he was introduced to us by my good pal Pete Morrell. Now Richard's father was a good tenor who sang in operas and musical shows around South Wales under the name of Clive Lemon. On one particular occasion, when visiting Richard, we witnessed a rare public event when Richard and his father sang a wonderful classical duet. At that time Richard was single and we had a conversation concerning him coming over to Florida where I would set him up with some gigs. Although he would only be playing for tips that money would be all his as he would be staying at our house at no cost, for the duration of his visit. He was, of course, a single man back then but that very quickly changed and in no time at all he had started a family and the rest, as they say, is history. So here we are years later, sitting in Florida and watching Richard doing his Billy Joel songs and my thought was, that in a way, he did in fact get to America but not actually in person. Apparently the Lewis' had heard Richard *the Piano Man* Harris' routine at another wedding function and liked him so much that they immediately hired him for their own upcoming event. This is just another time where a previous life experience has come back to haunt me. By the way the Lewis' are now owner/operators of De Courcey's Manor in the town of Pentyrch just north of Cardiff. I was invited to have a meal there on my recent visit and I can absolutely state, with my hand on my heart, the food is first class and I can think of no finer places in that whole region to hold a business conference or a family wedding. On a daily basis this establishment is run by the Lewis girls Rachel and Sarah.

Recently and once more at the Celtic Manor, the idol of Welsh rugby past, the iconic Gareth Edwards passed by the table that I was dining at. Just the glimpse of him was exciting to me as he was, without a doubt, one of the greatest players to ever strap on a pair of rugby boots. Recently, because it is the summer and there is no rugby being played at the present, on the Sky Sports television channel they have been showing bygone international rugby matches but none of them compare with, in my humble opinion, the greatest game of them all. The game I am referring to is when the Barbarians beat the New Zealand "All Blacks" team at Cardiff, in 1973, by twenty three points to eleven. At the halftime whistle the Barbarians were winning by an unheard of score, against the All Blacks, of seventeen points to zero and the southern hemisphere team did not know what had hit them. Not only was this probably the greatest rugby game ever played but during that match, in many people's opinion, the greatest try [touchdown] ever seen was scored. I believe the try started from a lineout and the opposition won the ball. As is their normal mode of play, their outside half launched a huge kick high into the air. This was fielded by a home team player who immediately gave the ball to Phil Bennett. He started to run to his right but then, with three audacious sidesteps, he beat three players and changed direction and sprinted to his left. On that side of the pitch was the whole set of Barbarian forwards who joined in as the move swept down field. I believe, if my memory serves me correctly, that everyone of them handled the ball in that attack. Just as the last forward was about to pass the ball to the left wing, up came Gareth. He ran at lightning speed inside of the wing and took the pass without even breaking stride. In a flash he sprinted down the touch line and dived over in the corner for a spectacular score. Quite often, when people reminisce, it is called *Gareth's Try* and everyone knows immediately what they are referring to. In truth, however, it was the whole team's try and I do believe that even that old war horse Willie John McBride had a hand in it. Some things in life have a habit of brightening up a dreary day and conjuring up the memory of this event is one of those never to be forgotten occasions. This will live on and be talked about in rugby circles for generations yet to come.

I have been told, at various stages of my life's development, that I have a complex mix of traits. For instance I, on my gentler side, love gardening and have around twenty or so flowers and plants in various rooms of my house. Yet, when it comes to playing sports I am fiercely competitive and will damage anyone who tries to hinder my progress. I have only attended, at the most, three funerals in my lifetime and in the last fifty years I have not even attended one. Perhaps

I am afraid of facing my own mortality but I think that it is more likely to be that I do not need to impress any of the other mourners and that the only one that I do care about has already departed. I try not to mix with older in-firmed people because all that they ever do is talk about all their ailments. I know that one day I will be in a similar situation myself but, until that time comes, I would prefer not to be thrown into that arena. This is the same reason why I rarely ever visit hospitals. I never ever was a member of a trade union and I think that this was because I grew up without a father and had to fight my own battles. On the other hand there is no doubt that I am, and always will be, a social butterfly. Maybe I naturally graduated to writing books because throughout my life I have always been inquisitive and asked a load of questions. When I meet a stranger who intrigues me I just have to know all about them. Their likes, there dislikes, what line of business they are in, where they are from, where they now live and so on and so on. Thank goodness I have a long memory and retain a good portion of everything that I am interested in which makes me able to pass such details onto others. This, to me, has proved to be a blessing in disguise and remember, in the words of the Fluid Druid, "Rehab is for quitters."

Lyn as Braveheart

Island Rowdies

a.k.a. The Crazy Gang

Rico Suave
Big Bad Damir
Chris the Turk
Hayward the Brave
Speedy Tim
Texas Toby
Spanky Wash
Pete the Greek
Two Touch Tony
Headband Zach
Kon Tiki Chris
Samurai Sato
Ski Knee Josh
Oliver the Terminator
Jumping Joel
Zoran Zee
Willer Kretz
Rio Bravo
Half Back Alex
Chico the Mex
Alta Ego
Straight A Steve
Sughi Knee
Little Messi
Young Nani
Side Step Sammy
Greg the Rocket Ross
Aaron Parkin
Alex the other Greek
The Austinator
Gary Gee
Syracuse Jon
No Name Bing
Killer Kretz
Orlando Steve
Ray St. Charles
Adam of Troy
Atlanta Robbie
Sharkey Clarke

And all the other soccer playing nuts who have visited our Island on vacation and have joined in with us at one of our games. .

Clarke Books
Catalog of Titles

by Lyn Clarke
Memoirs of a Welshman
Ramblings of a Welshman
Reflections of a Welshman
Amazing States
Echoes in My Mind

by Sharon Clarke
Mourning Redemption
Morgan's Crossing

by Rosemary Ling & Barbara Kingsmore
Maddie's Paradise Mountain

by Rosemary Ling
Disgraced

For more information about Clarke Books and full descriptions of
the above titles, visit our website at www.clarkebooks.net